FEATURES OF THIS BOOK

- 496 alphabetical entries on subjects of interest to home aquarists

- Descriptions of more than 358 freshwater and marine species, most illustrated in full color

- Descriptions and treatment of all common ailments to which tropical fish are subject

- Extensive articles on the care and maintenance of aquaria, breeding of tropical fish and use of aquatic plants

- Information on the competitive exhibition of tropical fish

- Comprehensive articles on the evolution, classification and anatomy of tropical fish

- Exhaustive information on the feeding of individual species and of tropical fish in general

The Dell Encyclopedia of
TROPICAL
FISH

by T. W. Julian

Illustrated by Norman Weaver

Published by
Dell Publishing Co., Inc.

An original work created and produced by
Vineyard Books, Inc.
159 East 64 Street
New York, New York 10021

Dell ® TM 681510, Dell Publishing Co., Inc.
Printed in Italy by Arnoldo Mondadori Editore, Sp A

Preface

No book on tropical aquarium fish and their care can be complete. With new species, subspecies, and hybrids turning up constantly, and with new information on earlier discoveries piling up apace, any book on the subject necessarily is to some extent outdated the moment it is published. To further complicate matters, the overwhelming majority of existing works on tropical fish, scientific treatises excepted, has been produced neither by trained observers nor professional researchers and writers, but by a motley of hobbyists, explorers, dilettantes, commercial dealers, breeders, and the like. While some of the literature thus produced is useful enough in its way, it is in large part unsystematic, contradictory, duplicative, cumbersome, and all too often patronizes either reader or subject. Moreover, the illustrations in many recent books, while of high aesthetic quality, convey little reliable information about their subjects.

This book hardly pretends to have done what far larger, more ambitious, and more costly volumes have failed to do. Within its own scope, however, no effort has been spared to make it the most comprehensive, accurate, useful, and manageable handbook available at a popular price. The aim has been not to include every species of tropical fish (an impossibility, as already noted), but to present a representative spectrum made up of nearly four hundred freshwater and marine fishes and other aquarium creatures, along with concise articles on the various taxonomic families under which virtually every known tropical fish can be found. Additionally, extensive articles are included on all major subjects of interest to tropical fish fanciers, along with shorter articles on many topics of lesser importance.

This is a book for laymen, not scientists. In the interest of readability and brevity, the technical detail required of a scientific work has been omitted. Whereas an ichthyologist doubtless would insist on precise metric measurements, for example, various species are described here in terms relative to their kind. Thus "large" or "small" fishes are so described only in the context of their taxonomic classification, with the result that a three-inch-long member of the family Cyprinodontidae (which is made up in general of diminutive fishes) might be termed "large," while a two-pound sea bass (whose close relatives may weigh half a ton) may be called "small."

Finally, a note on the illustrations. A number of quite stunning books on tropical fish, replete with color photographs, have been published over the past few years. Unfortunately, however (and contrary to popular notions of photographic probity), the camera—especially when it is concerned with underwater subjects—is not an altogether reliable tool. Reflection, refraction, poor or injudicious lighting, and a host of other factors may combine to convey a thoroughly misleading idea of a given fish's appearance, with unnatural highlights looking convincingly like body markings, with shadows cast by plants easily mistaken for stripes, and with ambiguity lurking everywhere. The artist Monet long ago demonstrated that a yellow haystack could look blue in certain circumstances, but the watercolor illustrations in this book were not conceived as Impressionist paintings, with inherent color modified by its surroundings. Rather, they are renderings of subjects as those subjects are known to be, and not as they are perceived to be at a given moment. In short, what we all agree to be a blue fish is portrayed as a blue fish, not a blue fish bathed in a red or yellow light.

RELATIVE SIZES OF TROPICAL FISH

In general, tropical fish grow larger in the wild than in captivity. In captivity, the size of a given specimen often is determined by the nature of its environment. There usually will be an appreciable difference, for example, in the sizes of two adult specimens taken from a single spawning but raised in aquaria of appreciably differing sizes or states of congestion. Sizes given in the table that follows roughly represent the smallest and largest species of the more common members of the various taxonomic families, as those species are found at maturity, in captivity, and in good condition. Species that grow to more than two feet in length are indicated by the figure: 24″→.

FAMILY	SIZE
Acanthuridae	7–18″
Anabantidae	2½–10″
Antennariidae	3–8″
Apogonidae	1½–6″
Atherinidae	2½–4″
Bagridae	4–6″
Balistidae	3½–20″
Blennidae	1½–4″
Bunocephalidae	4–6″
Callichthydae	4½–6″
Canthigasteridae	3½–8″
Centrarchidae	¾–6″
Centriscidae	3–4″
Chaetodontidae	3½–16″
Chandidae	1½–2¼
Channidae	8–12″
Characidae	1¼–10″
Cichlidae	2–10″
Cirrhitidae	3–5″
Cobitidae	2¾–8″
Congridae	24″→
Cyprinidae	1¼–12″
Cyprinodontidae	1¼–4″
Diodontidae	10–24″→
Doradidae	4–6″
Gasterosteidae	2–3″
Gobiidae	1½–4″
Gymnotidae	6–12″
Hemirhamphidae	2–3″
Holocentridae	5–18″
Labridae	3–24″→
Loricariidae	3–12″
Lutjanidae	12–24″→
Malapteruridae	6″
Mochokidae	3–8″
Monacanthidae	4–24″→
Mormyridae	6–10″
Mullidae	3¾–18″
Muraenidae	24″→
Nandidae	2½–4″
Opistognathidae	4″
Osteoglossidae	24″→
Ostraciidae	5–20″
Pantodontidae	4–6″
Pempheridae	3–6″
Pimelodidae	2–8″
Platacidae	10–20″
Poeciliidae	¾–5″
Pomacanthidae	4–20″
Pomacentridae	2½–12″
Pomadasidae	12–16″
Scaridae	12–24″→
Scatophagidae	4–16″
Scorpaenidae	7–12″
Serranidae	4–24″→
Siluridae	2½–4½″
Syngnathidae	4–10″
Tetraodontidae	2–17″
Theraponidae	6–12″
Zanclidae	12″

Clown Triggerfish:
One of the larger marine aquarium fish (F. Balistidae)

Neon Tetra:
One of the smallest and most popular freshwater fish (F. Characidae)

Oscar:
Among the largest of the Cichlids (F. Cichlidae)

Agassiz's Dwarf Cichlid:
A small member of Family Cichlidae (F. Cichlidae)

Unless specifically described as
being native to marine or brackish
waters, all species, genera, and
families described in this book are
found in freshwater habitats.

ACANTHURIDAE: the taxonomic family consisting of the numerous herbaceous reef-dwelling marine surgeonfishes (also called lancet-fishes, doctorfishes, tangs), whose distinguishing characteristics are horizontally flattened disc-shaped bodies, often with no clear line of demarcation at the bases of the dorsal and anal fins, and the forward-pointing, frequently poisonous spine(s) borne at the caudal base.

ACHYLA: *see* DISEASES OF TROPICAL FISH.

ACIDITY: *see* WATER.

ADIPOSE FIN: a small, fatty translucent fin characteristic of many tetras and some other species, and located between the dorsal and caudal fins.

ADONIS (*Lepidarchus adonis*): a small, easily bred spotted brown tetra that tends to lurk in shady spots. *Habitat:* Southern Ghana. *Diet:* Brine shrimp and other small live foods, granulated dry foods.

AENEUS CATFISH or **BRONZE CATFISH** (*Corydoras aeneus*): a small, perpetually busy brownish-bronze scavenger, the most popular of the armored catfishes. It is much prized for its docile nature, lively behavior, tidy habits, and

Aeneus Catfish

humorous aspect. *Habitat:* West Indies and most of South America. *Diet:* Dry foods, tank detritus, tubifex worms.

AERATOR or **AIRSTONE:** a porous underwater device through which air is forced by an electrically operated pump. The action of the resulting bubbles serves to agitate the water surface, allowing harmful gases to escape from the aquarium.

AFRICAN KNIFEFISH (*Xenomystus nigri*): A large silver-grey creature lacking both dorsal and caudal fins, it moves by rippling the anal fin that extends nearly the full length of its body. *Habitat:* Central and West Africa. *Diet:* Live foods. NOTE: Should not be kept in a community tank.

AFRICAN LEAF FISH (*Polycentropis abbreviata*): a small but voracious fish which, with its mottled

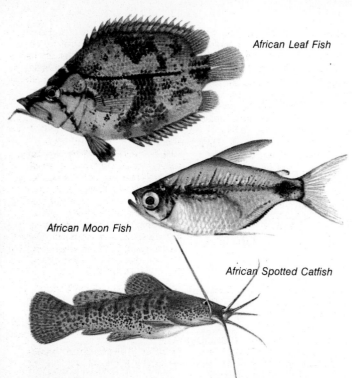

African Leaf Fish

African Moon Fish

African Spotted Catfish

brown body and almost invisible transparent tail, resembles a floating dead leaf. It is a natural predator with disproportionately large jaws and should be isolated from fishes smaller than itself, including members of its own species. An interesting breeder, it constructs its bubble-nests on the undersides of floating debris and spawns upward from an inverted position. *Habitat:* Equatorial West Africa. *Diet:* Earthworms, live smaller fish, chopped fresh animal organs.

AFRICAN MOON FISH (*Bathethiops fowleri*): a small, silver-blue

tetra that behaves well in community tanks but has not been bred in captivity. *Habitat:* Congo. *Diet:* Omniverous.

AFRICAN RED-FINNED BARB (*Barbodes camptacanthus*): a fairly large, warm-water barb, silvery with darker horizontal bands and, in the male and female respectively, reddish or yellowish dorsal and caudal fins. *Habitat:* Equatorial West Africa. *Diet:* Omniverous.

AFRICAN SPOTTED CATFISH (*Parauchenoglanis macrostoma*): Largely nocturnal and rather shy, this attractively marked orange-brown species has not been bred in captivity. *Habitat:* Equatorial West Africa. *Diet:* Live foods, frozen brine shrimp, and the like.

AFRICAN TETRA: popular designation for several tetra species, including *Alestes longipinnis, A. taeniurus, Nannaethiops tritaeniatus,* and *N. unitaeniatus.*

AFRICAN WHIPTAILED CATFISH (*Phractura ansorgei*): a shy, elongated, medium-sized catfish. It is red-brown with darker mottling and is easily bred. *Habitat:* Western and central tropical Africa. *Diet:* Small live foods and herbaceous matter.

AGASSIZ'S CATFISH (*Corydoras agassizai* or *C. ambiacus*): a small, attractively spotted yellow-brown bottom-feeder unbred in captivity. *Habitat:* Western Amazon River and vicinity. *Diet:* Scavenged matter, small live foods.

AGASSIZ'S DWARF CICHLID (*Apistogramma agassizai*): This is an easily bred, attractive little fish whose color varies according to its surroundings. The dorsal fin occupies most of its body length. Its tail is spade-shaped in the male, rounder in the female, and a dark band extends from stem to stern. *Habitat:* Central Amazon basin. *Diet:* Small live foods. NOTE: Males should be removed from pugnacious females after spawning.

AHL'S APHYOSEMION (*Aphyosemion calliurum ahli*): a small, strikingly marked, easily bred killie. Despite wide differences in general coloration, it is easily recognized by the bright yellow "fringe" on its fins. The fish coexists peacefully with other species, but may be quarrelsome with its own kind. *Habitat:* Equatorial West Africa. *Diet:* Small live foods.

AIRSTONE: *see* AERATOR.

ALBINISM: an absence of normal skin and fin pigmentation, sometimes accompanied by abnormally red eyes.

ALBINO: (1) A specimen characterized by ALBINISM. (2) Any of

Agassiz's Dwarf Cichlid

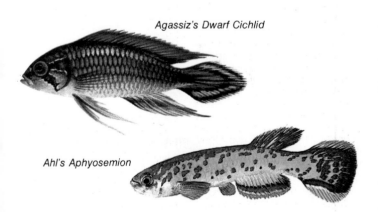

Ahl's Aphyosemion

13

several strains, such as the albino corydorus (*Corydorus aeneus*), deliberately bred from mutants. (3) Any of several species popularly but inaccurately considered to be marked by albinism, but whose pale coloration is the result of natural adaptation and not abnormal deficiencies.

ALGAE (singular: alga): any of various primitive and usually rootless, stemless, and leafless aquatic plants, most of them rich in chlorophyll and nutrients. In home aquaria they most commonly take the form of an unsightly green film or cloud caused by excessive natural illumination. Numerous tropical fishes, particularly fry and various types of catfish, feed on algae, as do many aquatic snails. Aside from its unsightliness, an immoderate incidence of algae should be avoided lest overcrowding cause the least hardy of the organisms to die and thereby foul the water with toxic substances. Excessive algae can be removed from the sides of aquaria with a variety of scrapers sold commercially, or with various nonmetallic scouring "wools." A yellowish cloudiness in aquaria usually indicates the presence of decaying algae and calls for an immediate and complete change of water.

ALKALINITY: *see* WATER.

AMAZON DWARF CICHLID (*Apistogramma pertense*): One of the most peaceable members of the cichlids, this small, rather nondescript fish breeds and rears its young with less ferocity than its near relatives. *Habitat:* Central Amazon basin. *Diet:* Varied, with small live foods preferred.

AMAZON SWORDPLANT (*Echinodorus paniculatus*): one of the most popular of the decorative aquatic PLANTS.

AMERICAN FLAGFISH (*Jordanella floridae*): a small, dull-green, semitropical cyprinodont more popular in Western Europe than its native United States. *Habitat:* Florida. *Diet:* Varied, but largely herbaceous.

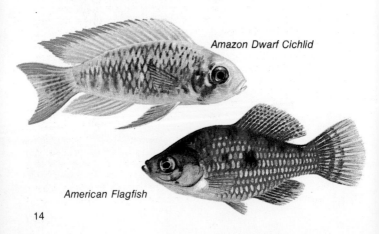

Amazon Dwarf Cichlid

American Flagfish

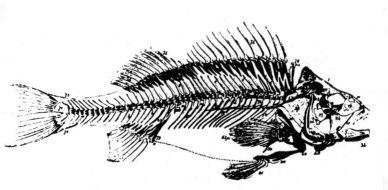

Bone structure of a perch done by the outstanding French anatomist Georges Cuvier in 1821. Space does not permit listing the names of the 81 bones shown above.

ANABANTIDAE: the taxonomic classification embracing the 38 known species of labyrinth fishes, all characterized by a distinctive respiratory LABYRINTH ORGAN that enables them to breathe atmospheric air. The gouramis, the climbing perch, and the betta, or Siamese fighting fish, belong to the family Anabantidae.

ANATOMY: All true fish are cold-blooded gill-breathing vertebrates, characteristically streamlined in shape and equipped with fins, skin, and mucous glands, usually bearing transparent scales or bony plates, and having no neck or other distinct separation between head and body. Within this generalized description, fishes may range in size from gobies 2/5 of an inch long to whale sharks some 50 feet in length, and in shape from the snakelike jawless lampreys of the class Agnatha to the vertically flattened broad soles of the family Achiridae to the horizontally flattened scats and monodactyls.

Most are oviparous, but some sharks and all members of the family Poeciliidae bring forth their young live. (*See also* REPRODUCTION.)

Most fishes are equipped with several membranous fins used for locomotion, stabilization, and directional change. These fins are usually either hard-rayed (*i.e.*, spiny) or soft-rayed, and the number of rays, hard or soft, in a given fish's finnage is a determinant factor in the identification of its species, as are certain longitudinal and transverse, or vertical, scale counts. A few species, such as the lung fishes of the family Lepidosirenidae, may also bear primitive, ropelike ventral and pectoral fins which function much as do a rowboat's oars. The number, placement, size, and shape of the fins varies from one fish to another, although the more closely related any two fishes are, the more similar their finnage is likely to be. Most fish are equipped with a single dor-

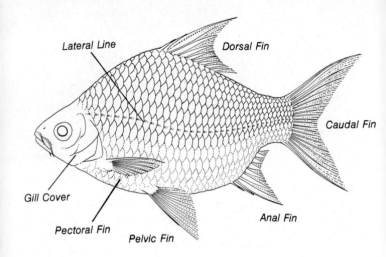

Lateral Line

Dorsal Fin

Caudal Fin

Gill Cover

Pectoral Fin

Pelvic Fin

Anal Fin

sal fin, but some, such as the various gobies and silversides, are endowed with two, one behind the other, while a few species, such as the AFRICAN KNIFEFISH (*Xenomystus nigri*) and certain selectively bred goldfish, bear no dorsal fins at all. Many characins, on the other hand, are endowed with a small, fatty fin—the adipose fin, situated between the dorsal and caudal fins—that is absent in most other fishes. The various angelfishes and some similar species flaunt magnificently elongated pelvic fins, while others, notably the puf-

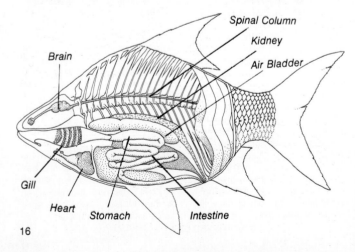

Brain

Spinal Column

Kidney

Air Bladder

Gill

Heart

Stomach

Intestine

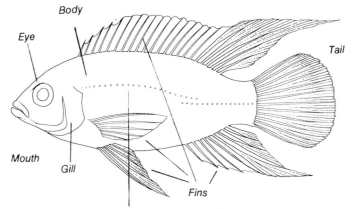

Body

Eye

Tail

Mouth

Gill

Fins

Broken horizontal line is called
lateral line.

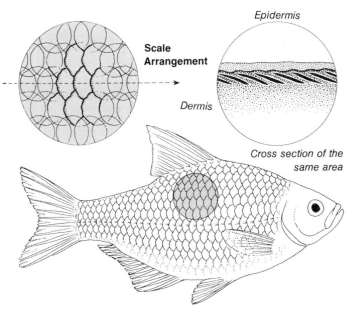

Scale Arrangement

Epidermis

Dermis

Cross section of the
same area

Scale layout of a typical fish

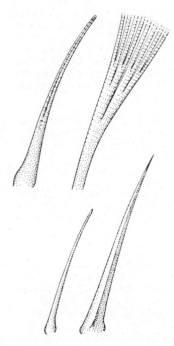

Four typical finray structures

fers, lack even the most rudimentary pelvic fins. A very few species, the aforementioned African Knifefish for example, even lack caudal, or tail, fins, but all true fish have at least one fin of some sort, with most species bearing several, with such members as the ventral, pectoral, and pelvic fins laterally paired.

Naturally, the external appearance of the different fishes is determined above all by the skeletal structure, which is either bony, as is the case in the vast majority of species, or cartilaginous, as it is in

the sharks, rays, and skates. The internal organs generally vary somewhat in size and shape, depending on a given fish's configuration, but otherwise are similar in makeup, consisting of heart, liver, kidney, stomach, intestine, closely connected reproductive and excretory systems, and, in all but a very few species, a swim bladder whose precise function is somewhat conjectural, but which generally is believed to be a stabilizing and auditory organ. The skin consists of a thick dermal layer, which produces both scales and the protective mucous that covers the body, and a thinner epidermis.

A few primitive species, comprising the family Lepidosirenidae, breathe by means of lungs, while some forty species that comprise the family Anabantidae are equipped with a LABYRINTH ORGAN through which they breathe atmospheric air. The vast majority of fish, however, breathe by taking water in through their mouths and passing it through their gills, where thin-walled capillaries absorb its oxygen and from which carbon dioxide waste is expelled.

In the reproductive process (*see* also REPRODUCTION), eggs are discharged from the female's ovary and are expelled through the oviduct and urogenital sinus. The male's sperm is discharged from the testis through the vas deferens, seminal vesicle, and urogenital sinus.

ANCHOR WORM: *see* DISEASES OF TROPICAL FISH.

ANEMONE: any of numerous marine invertebrates of the phylum Coelenterata and class Anthozoa, having a flowerlike structure, a flexible cylindrical body, a saclike internal cavity, and tentacles surrounding a central mouth. The striking coloration of numerous sea anemones, their bizarre appearance, and their seemingly anomalous nature (they are commonly mistaken for carnivorous plants) combine to make them very popular with marine aquarists. Anemones are fragile, however, and should not be mishandled or kept in community tanks by novices. Moreover, they can be dangerous to some of the smaller marine fishes. *Habitat:* Tropical marine waters throughout the world. *Diet:* Shredded raw shrimp. NOTE: Because of the anemone's lack of mobility, food should be dropped directly into its open tentacles and uneaten fragments should not be allowed to accumulate in the aquarium.

ANEMONE FISH or **DAMSELFISH** or **DEMOISELLE:** any of numerous marine species, many of them extremely popular with home aquarists, that comprise family POMACENTRIDAE. They include the BLUE DAMSELFISH and the CLOWN ANEMONE.

ANGELFISH (*Pterophyllum scalare, P. altum,* and *P. eimekei*): Because of their striking appearance, graceful shape, and rather stately carriage, these are among the best-known and most popular of the cichlids in particular and tropical fishes in general. These sizable creatures are characterized by their arrow-shaped bodies, elongated dorsal and anal fins, and tendrillike pelvic fins. In the most characteristic species, the fish is clearly marked with three vertical bands, one of which runs through

Angelfish

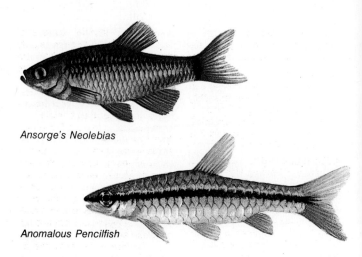

Ansorge's Neolebias

Anomalous Pencilfish

the eye. Many hybrids exist, however, and often are distinguishable only by experts. Most angelfish are peaceful and well-suited to community aquaria, thus further enhancing their popularity. They breed easily in captivity. *Habitat:* the Amazon and Orinoco Rivers and their tributaries and environs. *Diet:* Live and frozen foods, minced beef heart, and (for fry) finely powdered dry foods.

ANGLERFISH (*Antennarius scaber*): A relatively scarce and highly unusual marine fish, this curious creature "walks" about the bottom in search of its food, changing color to match its environment, and then actually fishes for its prey with a rod and lure attached to its nose. *Habitat:* Florida coastal waters. *Diet:* Live minnows, unwanted fry.

ANOMALOUS PENCILFISH (*Nannostomus anomalus*): a quite small, very attractive characin bearing a black lateral stripe (and a less discernible gold stripe) on its

yellow-tan body, and with red anal and lower caudal fins. *Habitat:* Central portion of the northern third of South America. *Diet:* Varied, with live foods preferred.

ANSORGE'S NEOLEBIAS (*Neolebias ansorgei*): a small, rather uncharacteristic tetra lacking an adipose fin. Its green-and-gold coloration fades quickly in uncomfortable surroundings. *Habitat:* Central Africa. *Diet:* Small live foods. NOTE: Extremely water-sensitive; requires soft aged water and warm temperatures.

ANTENNARIIDAE: the taxonomic family comprising the marine frog-fishes or anglerfishes, most of which are equipped with limblike pectoral and pelvic fins and extraordinarily capacious mouths and stomachs, and many of which are elaborately camouflaged to resemble living or dead flora, or endowed with rodlike appendages with which prey is lured toward their mouths.

APHYOSEMION: any of a genus of egg-laying tooth carps of the family Cyprinodontidae.

APOGONIDAE: the taxonomic family comprising the marine cardinal fishes, characteristically small in size, large-eyed, and bearing two separate and dissimilar dorsal fins, the second of which is symmetrical with the anal fin.

AQUARIUM CARE AND MANAGEMENT: Samuel Pepys, who in 1665 wrote that "fishes kept in a glass of water . . . will live for ever," may have been the first, but was hardly the last, Western observer to overrate the durability of tropical fish. In nature, most species of tropical fish are well equipped to survive in highly competitive environments. In captivity, however, where the concern is not so much with the survival of species as of individual specimens, some care must be taken to provide a healthful, protective environment in which various specimens, whether of the same or differing species, peacefully can coexist.

With the relatively recent development of easily-shaped one-piece plastic aquaria, the tropical fish hobbyist has a wide range of options to choose from as far as the sizes and proportions of fish tanks are concerned. Most experienced aquarists, however, continue to prefer relatively shallow rectangular glass-and-metal tanks, for their greater rigidity, optimum surface areas and the minimal visual distortion of their contents. Since water is an extremely heavy substance (at normal temperatures, a cubic foot weighs about 62 lbs.) and both glass and plastics are flexible, aquaria of appreciable size require sturdy frames, which traditionally are constructed of metal bars bent at right angles and treated so that corrosion, rust and like chemical deterioration cannot affect the purity of the water they contain.

In general, susceptibility to carbon monoxide poisoning diminishes in inverse ratio to the surface of the aquarium, although such devices as electrically-driven filters and aerators allow for a heavier incidence of fish than ordinarily would be possible in a tank whose life-support system was not mechanically augmented. Whatever the size of the tank and its population, though, overcrowding always should be avoided and hygienic conditions should be maintained. A healthy fish tank is a clean tank, with actively circulating water, adequate filtration, proper oxygenization, and as little accumulation as possible of such organic and non-organic wastes as decaying foodstuffs and artificial chemicals.

For both aesthetic and practical purposes, most home aquarists plant their fish tanks with live aquatic or amphibious vegetation. Except when the various species of floating plants are used exclusively, the introduction of live plants requires the prior introduction of compost, i.e., the medium on the tank bed, usually a fine-textured gravel (which may or may not be spread over peat), in which the plants can take root.

Overleaf: *A healthy, well-planted community aquarium.*

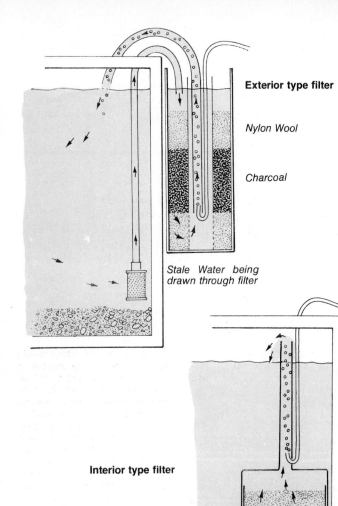

Exterior type filter

Nylon Wool

Charcoal

Stale Water being drawn through filter

Interior type filter

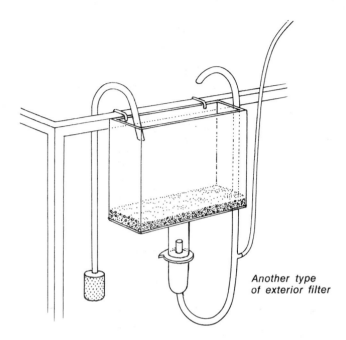

Another type of exterior filter

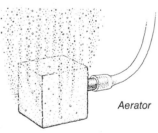

Aerator

Ideally, such gravel is light in color and fine enough in texture to keep organic material from penetrating its surface too deeply, but not so fine as to allow unsightly detritus to accumulate on the surface. To avoid clouding the water, the use of peat or similar bases is inadvisable in conjunction with species of fish that tend to feed upon or uproot plants.

Theoretically, a fish tank should be a self-supporting system in which plants, activated by natural light, draw nutrients from the compost and provide themselves and other organisms with the needs of their respiratory systems. In practice, however, a host of variables tend to upset this very delicate natural balance, and most commercial and home aquarists therefore prefer controlled artificial light to unpredictable natural light, thermostatically controlled water temperatures to the variables of room temperature, and so on. Moreover, artificial lighting not only inhibits the buildup of algae (which are both unsightly and potentially toxic in uncontrolled numbers), but usually is more aesthetically satisfying as a display medium for tropical fish whose color and iridescence tend to be obscured by natural light. Ten hours of 25-watt incandescent illumination per square foot of water surface per day, or the equivalent thereof, generally is considered adequate for average home aquaria, and most aquarium lighting takes the form of bulbs or flourescent tubes affixed to the undersides of hoods or covers that serve to mask the glare and to keep the fish from leaping out of the tank.

Since water, as has been noted, is an extremely heavy substance, tank frames alone, however sturdy, usually are not sufficient in themselves to provide enough rigidity to insure that an aquarium will remain free of leaks. Aquaria therefore should be mounted on specially constructed metal stands, shelves or other perfectly flat, rigid supports and, once so mounted, should be moved as little as possible. Before the introduction of fish, plants, etc., the tank should be filled with water and inspected for leakage. Should leaks be discovered, the offending spots should be well marked and, after the tank has been drained and allowed to dry thoroughly, caulked with any of several commercially available non-toxic compounds.

In general, tropical aquaria should be maintained at temperatures ranging from 65° F to 85° F, depending on the needs of the species of fish they house. To control these temperatures, either an internal or external thermostat, both electrically operated, both inexpensive and both readily available at aquarists' supply houses, should be obtained and installed.

The thermostat, together with an electric pump (which activates both the tank's filtration and aeration systems), filter and aerator, comprise the equipment essential to a non-self-supportive aquarium. Filters, like thermostats, can be mounted on the inside or outside of the tank, although most aquarists perfer external devices for aesthetic reasons, and consist of a container of glass or plastic filled with charcoal, nylon wool or similar substances that trap foreign matter as the aquarium water is electrically pumped through the filtration medium.

Although many aquarists introduce live snails into their fish tanks to keep tank sides free of algae, these creatures are not necessary components of a well-maintained environment and indeed often turn out to be a source of pollution when they die unobserved in their shells. Should algae accumulate on tank surfaces, simple and inexpensive scrapers, obtainable at all aquarium supply shops, will quickly eliminate them.

Once an aquarium has been provided with compost and mechanical equipment, filled with water and planted (a simple device known as a planting stick facilitates this operation), it should be allowed to operate for a week or so before fish are introduced into it. The space requirements of fish vary according to species and the size of individual specimens. As a rule of thumb, 25 to 30 square inches of water surface should be alloted to each small-to-average-size fish in a community tank and overcrowding never should be allowed to occur.

Archer Fish

Arnold's Characin

ARCHER FISH (*Toxotes jaculator*): This is a good-sized, silvery-yellow fish with a yellow caudal fin and six vertical black bands, one of which runs through the eye. It is renowned for its ability to "shoot down" insect prey by expelling beads of water from its mouth with considerable force and for its remarkable ability to compensate for visual refraction when aiming its shots. *Habitat:* India, Southeast Asia, East Indies. *Diet:* Insect prey, minced meat. NOTE: Requires slightly brackish water.

ARGULUS: *see* DISEASES OF TROPICAL FISH.

ARIPIRANGA PENCILFISH (*Nannostomus aripirangensis*): A close relative of the anomalous pencilfish, it is brown with a black lateral stripe and red ventral fins. *Habitat:* Lower Amazon River. *Diet:* Varied, with small live foods preferred.

ARMORED CATFISH (*Callichthys callichthys*): This medium-sized, greenish-to-dun-colored, voracious creature has a taste for live fish. It tends to uproot small plants and generally reduce aquaria to varying states of disarray. It bears heavy overlapping plates on much of its body and is quite lively. *Habitat:* West Indies and much of South America. *Diet:* Live foods.

ARNOLD'S CHARACIN or **RED-EYED CHARACIN** (*Arnoldichthys spilopterus*): a small, silvery African tetra rarely, if ever, bred in captivity. *Habitat:* Equatorial West Africa. *Diet:* Varied.

ARNOLD'S KILLIE (*Epiplatys dageti monroviae*): a small, attractively marked yellow-green specimen with orange markings in the vicinity of the throat. Somewhat aggressive in community tanks.

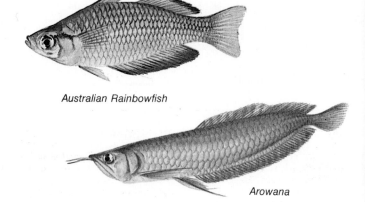

Australian Rainbowfish

Arowana

Habitat: Liberia. *Diet:* Small live foods.

ARNOLD'S LYRETAIL (*Aphyosemion arnoldi*): A small, strikingly handsome killie, it bears vivid red markings on a blue-green body, and (in the male) a slightly attenuated caudal fin. It does not get along well in community tanks and prefers a well-planted aquarium. *Habitat:* Mouth of the Niger River. *Diet:* Small live foods.

ARNOLD'S SUCKER CATFISH (*Otocinclus arnoldi*): This small, peaceful scavenger has a gray-brown body marked with a transverse dark stripe. *Habitat:* La Plata River region between Uruguay and Argentina. *Diet:* Algae, tubifex worms.

AROWANA (*Osteoglossum bicirrhosum*): A survivor of the Jurassic era, this relatively large, serpentlike fish is easily tamed but voracious and should be raised in isolation. Its capacious jaws are embellished with a spikelike pair of "chin whiskers" and its greenish-gray body with well-defined scales. *Habitat:* Amazon River and its environs. *Diet:* Live fish, raw shrimp.

ARROWHEAD TETRA (*Gephyrocharax caucanus*): a small, hyperactive characin whose color varies to suit its surroundings. It is best kept in schools. *Habitat:* Colombia. *Diet:* Varied, with live foods preferred.

ATHERINIDAE: the taxonomic family made up of the so-called silversides, basically coastal saltwater fishes, several species of which have adapted to fresh water. The AUSTRALIAN RAINBOWFISH (*Melanoptaenia nigrans*) is one of the best known of the silversides.

AUSTRALIAN RAINBOWFISH (*Melanotaenia nigrans*): A fairly sizable, easily kept yellow-green fish, it is most readily distinguishable by its two dorsal fins. *Habitat:* Australia. *Diet:* Varied.

BADIS or **DWARF CHAMELEON FISH** (*Badis badis*): a shy, small-mouthed nandid with highly changeable coloration and markings. *Habitat:* India. *Diet:* Small live foods. NOTE: If kept in a community tank, shelters and hiding places should be provided.

BAGRIDAE: the taxonomic family embracing numerous nonarmored Old World catfishes similar in their external appearance to the South American catfishes of family PIMELODIDAE.

BALA SHARK (*Balantiocheilus melanopterus*): a large, attractively marked, peaceful fish with a prominent dorsal fin (hence the "shark"). All of the fins are yellow with a broad black edge. A good scavenger, it is also a good jumper and must be kept in a covered tank. *Habitat:* Thailand, Malay Archipelago. *Diet:* Live foods, aquarium detritus.

BALISTIDAE: the taxonomic family comprising the marine triggerfishes, so called for the characteristic first spine of their dorsal fins, a protective mechanism that "locks" in an erect position when the smaller spines behind it are erected. (*See also* CLOWN TRIGGERFISH and QUEEN TRIGGERFISH.)

BANDED BUTTERFLY FISH (*Chaetodon striatus*): a strikingly marked marine fish with vertical black stripes on a silver-white body. It is distinctly spade-shaped, as are other butterfly fishes.

Banded Butterfly Fish

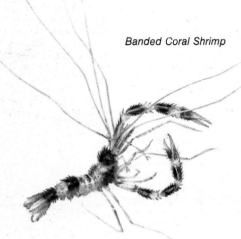

Banded Coral Shrimp

Habitat: Coastal Florida southward to Puerto Rico. *Diet:* Tubifex and other small worms augmented by occasional brine shrimp. NOTE: A difficult feeder that often starves in captivity.

BANDED CORAL SHRIMP (*Stenopus hispidus*): Very popular with marine aquarists, this striking crustacean has a red-and-white candy-striped body. It breeds readily and gets along well in community tanks, although it periodically becomes vulnerable to injury between the shedding of its old shell and the growth of a new one. *Habitat:* Tropical Atlantic and Pacific waters. *Diet:* Chopped fish, shrimp and worms, algae, parasites scavenged from the skin of various fishes.

BANDED CYNOLEBIAS (*Cynolebias adloffi*): Like other members of the *Cynolebias* genus, this aggressive little egg-burier has an abbreviated life cycle, for in its natural state it lives in ponds that evaporate during the dry season; the previously burried eggs remain dormant, later to hatch when the ponds are restored by heavy rains. Because of its short life span and the male's combative nature, it is not popular with hobbyists, although it is easily bred in conditions that artificially approximate those that occur in its natural habitat. (A bed of peat moss is removed from the aquarium bottom after spawning has been completed, stored in a semidry state for several weeks, then returned to soft, acid water: the eggs hatch within hours.) Males are yellow-brown with dark vertical bands and pale blue fins; the smaller females are quite drab. *Habitat:* Southern Brazil. *Diet:* Small live foods.

BANDED KNIFE FISH or **SARAPO** (*Gymnotus carapo*): Like the knife fishes in general, this good-sized, reddish, handsomely marked nocturnal species lacks dorsal and caudal fins. The rippling motion of its elongated anal fin provides its motive power. An aggressive predator, it should not be kept in a community tank. *Habitat:* Central America to southern Uruguay. *Diet:* Small live fish, chopped fresh shrimp, beef heart.

BANDED LEPORINUS (*Leporinus fasciatus*): a very popular, good-sized, and vividly marked yellow fish with evenly spaced vertical black bands. It is something of a headstander, spending much of its time foraging on the bottom for algae or other vegetable matter. It behaves well toward other species but will eat decorative plants and jump out of uncovered tanks. *Habitat:* Most of South America. *Diet:* Mixed, but largely herbaceous.

BANDED LIMIA (*Limia vittata* or *Poecilia vittata*): An avid vegetarian with a marked preference for algae, this somewhat randomly spotted yellow-green fish cannot be described with much accuracy as "banded." The female is much larger than the male, which usually attains a length of about 2½ inches. *Habitat:* Cuba. *Diet:* Extremely varied, but preferably herbaceous.

BANDED LOACH (*Botia hymenophysa*): A light reddish-brown creature handsomely marked with a series of well-defined vertical bands, this good-sized loach is active, but mostly nocturnal. It is a useful scavenger in a community tank, but is not to be trusted with smaller fishes. *Habitat:* Malay Peninsula, Indonesia, and much of the Malay Archipelago. *Diet:* Live foods, unwanted small fish, food scraps left by tankmates. NOTE: Should be kept in clear, well-agitated water.

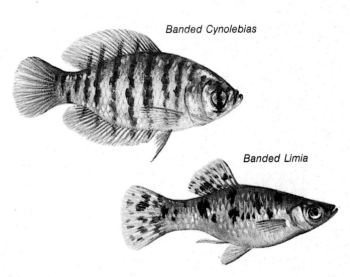

Banded Cynolebias

Banded Limia

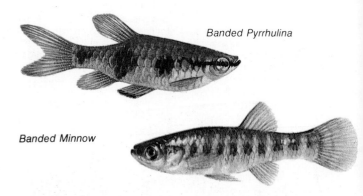

Banded Pyrrhulina

Banded Minnow

BANDED MINNOW (*Aphanius fasciatus*): a small, easily-bred fish with a preference for slightly brackish water. White-bellied with a dull green back shading off to blue-green on the sides, it is marked with a darker irregular lateral stripe and a series of silver-blue vertical bands. *Habitat:* Mediterranean littoral. *Diet:* Small live foods and herbaceous matter.

BANDED PYRRHULINA (*Pyrrhulina vittata*): a peaceful little fish saddled with a misnomer—it is not banded but bears three indistinct spots on its light-brown body and a thin horizontal line on the side of its head. A good mixer in community tanks. *Habitat:* Northern Brazil, around the juncture of the Amazon and Tapajoz Rivers. *Diet:* Varied, with small live foods preferred.

BARB: any member of the genera *Barbodes, Capoeta,* and *Puntius,* of which some of the commonest varieties are the tiger, cherry, rosy, two-spot, ruby, tinfoil, and checkered barbs. Generally lively, easily bred little creatures, they can be annoying in community tanks, because of their fin-nipping pro-clivities, but are quite popular among aquarists, if not among other fishes.

BARBEL: a slender, whiskerlike sensory organ borne on the snouts, lips, or jaws of certain fishes, particularly catfishes, usually in one or more pairs.

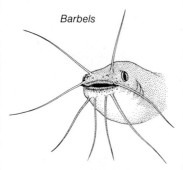

Barbels

BARBER'S TETRA (*Mimagoniates barberi*): A small, active characin with a brown body and darker horizontal stripe, it prefers strong natural light and oxygen-rich water. *Habitat:* Paraguay and bordering regions of Brazil and Argentina. *Diet:* Small live foods.

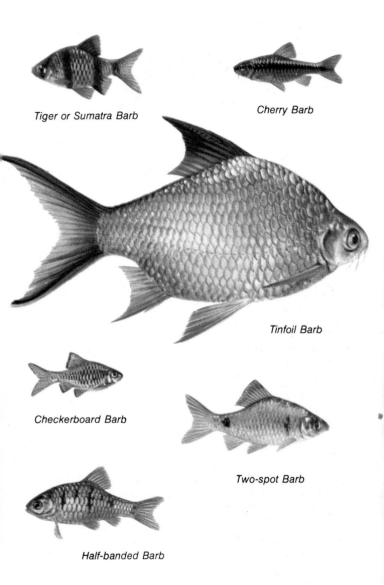

Tiger or Sumatra Barb

Cherry Barb

Tinfoil Barb

Checkerboard Barb

Two-spot Barb

Half-banded Barb

Batfish

Nannostomus e.): a small, lively, brownish fish with a silver belly and sides marked with five more or less diagonal dark bars. *Habitat:* British Guiana. *Diet:* Varied. NOTE: Should be kept in a covered tank.

BARRED SQUIRRELFISH: *see* SQUIRRELFISH.

BATFISH: the popular name for such large Pacific marine fishes as *Platax pinnatus* and *P. orbicularis*, and for a number of fish from Atlantic waters which bear them no resemblance. *Platax p.*, a spectacular jet-black creature with red edgings, and the yellow-brown *Platax o.* bear unusually large dorsal fins and make extremely graceful additions to saltwater aquaria, where they live well on unwanted small fish and fry. The Atlantic batfishes, which rarely are available to hobbyists, resemble the ANGLERFISH (*Antennarius scaber*).

BEAUFORT'S LOACH (*Botia beauforti*): A large, nocturnally active gray-green fish with a dark-banded back and dotted sides, it behaves well in community tanks provided it can find seclusion. *Habitat:* Thailand. *Diet:* Varied, with live foods and scavenged material preferred.

BEAU GREGORY (*Pomacentrus leucostictus*): a small, hardy, jewellike marine fish, colored a vivid blue and sulphur-yellow and fond of hiding in coral. Some larger specimens can be aggressive, but most get along well if properly introduced into community tanks. Particularly attractive when raised in schools. *Habitat:* Florida coastal waters, West Indies. *Diet:* Varied, with green algae indicated periodi-

BARRED LOACH: the common name shared by *Botia lucas-bahi* and *Neomacheilus fasciatus*. The former, grayish-green, nocturnal and native to Thailand, lives well in a community tank, but the latter, brown, yellow-banded, and found in the Malay Archipelago, does not. *Diet* (for both): Mixed, with live worms preferred.

BARRED PENCILFISH (*Poecilobrycon espei, Nannobrycon e.* or

Beau Gregory

Beira Nothobranch

cally. NOTE: Fry are extremely vulnerable to shock.

BEIRA NOTHOBRANCH (*Nothobranchius melanospilus*): a small, voracious EGG-BURIER of which the male, with its red-edged scales and blue-edged red fins, is by far the more distinctive. Like the South American *cynolebias* species, it is an "annual" fish that does not survive the dry season in its natural habitat. *Habitat:* Southeastern Africa. *Diet:* Small live foods.

BENEDENIA: *see* DISEASES OF TROPICAL FISH.

BERTHOLD'S KILLIE (*Aphyosemion bertholdi*): An EGG-BURIER, males of this species are blue-green and are attractively marked with red spots and, on their fins, stripes. Females are a nondescript brown. Small killies, they prefer their own kind. *Habitat:* Liberia. *Diet:* Small live foods.

BETTA or **SIAMESE FIGHTING FISH** (*Betta splendens*): One of the best-known and most spectacular of the freshwater tropical fishes, in its natural "unimproved" state it is a rather drab, short-finned creature resembling BREDER'S BETTA (*B. brederi*). Through selective breeding, however, it has developed a stunning range of coloration and unnaturally long, flowing anal, dorsal, and caudal fins. In Thailand, the males are prized for their ferocity and are pitted against one another much as fighting cocks are in Latin America, with wagers placed on the outcome of the fight. Their intramural aggressiveness notwithstanding, they get along well with most other species of comparable size (2-3 inches) and often can be stroked when they surface for air. They are easily bred and live well

35

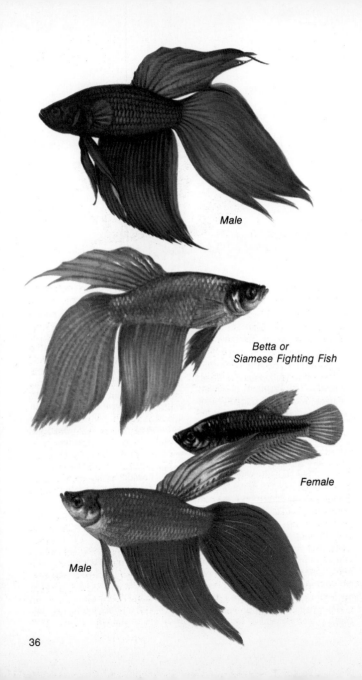

Male

*Betta or
Siamese Fighting Fish*

Female

Male

36

Black Angelfish

in very little space. *Habitat:* Indo-China, Malay Peninsula. *Diet:* All nonherbaceous foods.

BIG-EYED CICHLID (*Acaronia nassa*): a sizable, ferocious, rather unattractive creature that cannot be kept in community tanks and consequently is not very popular with aquarists. *Habitat:* Northern Amazon River and its tributaries. *Diet:* Varied raw meaty foods and live fish.

BLACK ACARA or **PORT ACARA** (*Aequidens portalegrensis*): Very popular and easily bred, this greenish-brown cichlid bears a dark spot amidships at about eye-level. Well behaved in community tanks, so long as its neighbors are too large to be preyed upon, but tends to disturb composts and uproot plants. *Habitat:* Central South America. *Diet:* Live foods, chopped meats, shrimp, in generous quantities.

BLACK ANGELFISH or **GRAY ANGELFISH** (*Pomacanthus arcuatus*): This magnificently marked marine fish is at its breathtaking best when kept small. When larger, its phosphorescent yellow and velvety, jet-black vertical alternations and startling blue pelvic fins begin to dull. The size of the individual specimen is governed more so than is usual by the dimensions of its tank and may range from a mere ½ inch to 16 inches or more in length. *Habitat:* Western Atlantic from Florida to Brazil. *Diet:* Varied, with live brine shrimp preferred for fry and smaller specimens and chopped (or even whole) earthworms for larger ones. The addition of paprika to its diet is said to heighten the fish's color.

BLACK AROWANA (*Osteoglossum ferreirai*): This voracious Brazilian curiosity is laterally banded with black and gold markings at birth, but gradually turns a uniform blue-black as it matures. Easily agitated, it cannot be kept with species small enough to be swallowed. *Habitat:* Northwestern Brazil. *Diet:* Small live fish.

37

BLACK-BARRED LIVEBEARER (*Quintana atrizona*): a very small, rather colorless fish. The female, at about 1½ inches, is twice the size of her mate, which is endowed with an unusually long, hooked gonopodium. *Habitat:* Cuba. *Diet:* Most foods in small particles.

BLACK-FINNED PEARL FISH or **DWARF ARGENTINE PEARL-FISH** (*Cynolebias nigripinnis*): Of the various egg-burying "annual" fishes, the male of this species is one of the most striking, with its starry pattern of pale dots on a deep black ground. Small, but very active sexually, it dislikes life in community aquaria. *Habitat:* Northeastern Argentina. *Diet:* Small live foods.

BLACK FLAG: *see* ROSY TETRA.

BLACK GHOST (*Apteronotus albifrons* or *Sternarchus albifrons*): Unlike other knife fishes, this large, amiable, easily-tamed creature bears rudimentary dorsal and caudal fins. Considered sacred by some Indians, it is seldom trapped and relatively rare and costly. *Habitat:* Northern Brazil, Surinam. *Diet:* Varied.

BLACK-LINED TETRA (*Hyphessobrycon scholzei*): a popular little fish whose silver-blue body is marked by a black stripe that runs from gill to tail. It is easily bred and adapts well to community tanks. *Habitat:* Para Federal District, northern Brazil. *Diet:* Varied.

BLACK SHARK (*Morulius chrysophekadion*): a large, primarily herbivorous scavenger that gets along better with other species than with members of its own. It is prized for its dark, graceful silhouette and its eagerness to keep aquaria free of algae. *Habitat:* Thailand. *Diet:* Varied, but mostly herbaceous.

BLACK-SPOT BARB (*Puntius filamentosus*): a good-sized, red-finned barb with a golden back and silvery sides and belly. It takes its popular name from a distinctive,

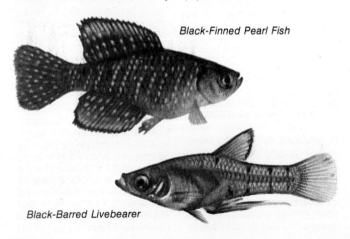

Black-Finned Pearl Fish

Black-Barred Livebearer

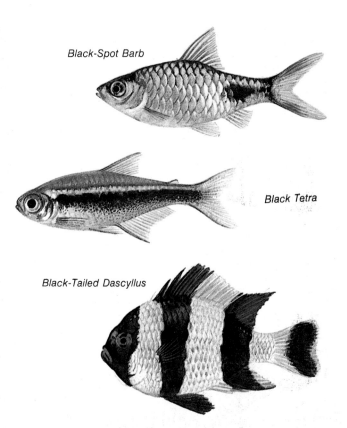

Black-Spot Barb

Black Tetra

Black-Tailed Dascyllus

slightly elongated black spot near the caudal fin. *Habitat:* India, Burma, Sri Lanka. *Diet:* Omnivorous, with a fondness for herbaceous matter.

BLACK-TAILED DASCYLLUS or **BLACK-TAILED HUMBUG** (*Dascyllus melanurus*): a small, attractive, white marine damselfish emphatically marked with four more or less evenly spaced black bands, of which one runs through the eye while another occupies the caudal

extremity. *Habitat:* Indo-Pacific waters west of Hawaii. *Diet:* Varied, with small live crustaceans preferred.

BLACK TETRA: either of two small, similar characins, (1) *Gymnocorymbus ternetzi* or (2) *Gymnocorymbus thayeri*, of which the former is characterized by much darker markings than the somewhat pallid latter. Hardy and easily bred, both are popular with aquarists. *Habitat:* (1) Central

South America; (2) Colombia, Upper Amazon region, Bolivia. *Diet:* (both) Varied, with small live foods preferred.

BLEEDING HEART TETRA or **TETRA PEREZ** (*Hyphessobrycon rubrostigma*): a good-sized characin whose tan body glows with a bluish sheen. It bears a pink dorsal fin boldly marked with a black spot. A very active, easily bred fish, it prefers a roomy tank. *Habitat:* Colombia. *Diet:* Varied, with small live foods preferred.

BLENNIIDAE: the loose taxonomic family comprising several related families of marine fishes popularly called "blennies" and most commonly belonging to the family Clinidae (the scaled blennies) or to the family Blenniidae (the scaleless blennies) itself.

BLENNY: any of numerous marine species belonging to the family BLENNIIDAE, the family Clinidae, or several less-known taxonomic categories.

BLIND CAVE CHARACIN or **BLIND CAVEFISH** (*Anoptichthys jordani*): Eyeless as a result of its long-standing preference for the total darkness of a subterranean environment, this medium-sized, somewhat etiolated fish is not altogether popular with those who are squeamish. It makes a useful addition to the community tank where it will forage expertly for food left uneaten by sighted fish. *Habitat:* Central Mexico. *Diet:* Small live and dry foods, scavenged material.

BLOODFIN (*Aphyocharax rubripinnis*): a small, very popular characin with a blue-gray body and blood-red fins. Active and best kept in schools, it gets along well with other species. *Habitat:* Parana River Argentina. *Diet:* Varied. NOTE: Thrives on frequent feedings.

BLOWFISH: any of numerous members of family TETRAODONTIDAE.

BLUE ACARA (*Aequidens pulcher*): a good-sized, somewhat pugnacious cichlid bearing rows of light-blue spots on a blue-gray or gray-brown body. It breeds easily and is known for its longevity, but is

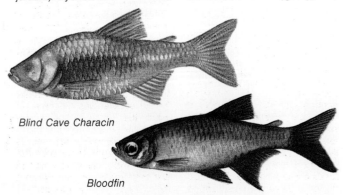

Blind Cave Characin

Bloodfin

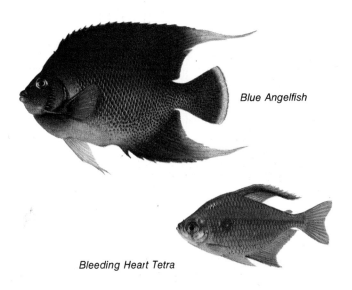

Blue Angelfish

Bleeding Heart Tetra

destructive of plants and smaller fishes. *Habitat:* Central America, Trinidad, northern South America. *Diet:* Live foods, chopped animal organs.

BLUE ANGELFISH (*Angelichthys cilaris*): Perhaps the best known of the marine angelfish common to the Atlantic, it should not be confused with the Pacific Blue Angelfish (*Pomacanthus semicirculatus*), a much rarer and more spectacularly marked creature. A welcome addition to community aquaria, it should not be kept with other blue angelfish of the same size. *Habitat:* Florida coastal waters. *Diet:* For smaller fish and fry, live brine shrimp in constant supply, finely chopped fresh and dry foods; for larger specimens, chopped or whole earthworms, depend-

ing on fish's capacity, coarsely chopped shrimp, lean meats, with the addition of paprika for color tone.

BLUE-BANDED NEOLEBIAS (*Neolebias landgrafi*): Very similar in appearance and habits to *Neolebias ansorgei,* it has a pale blue body as opposed to its relative's green body. *Habitat:* Nigeria. *Diet:* Small live foods.

BLUE CALLIURUM (*Aphyosemion calliurum calliurum*): a small, hardy egg-hanging species, of which the female is easily mistaken for AHL'S APHYOSEMION, while the male whose body color is shaded from light blue above to tan below, is more distinctively marked with red streaks. *Habitat:* Western Africa. *Diet:* Small live foods.

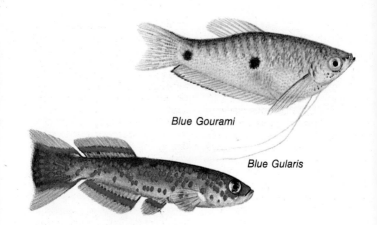

Blue Gourami

Blue Gularis

BLUE DEMOISELLE or **BLUE DAMSELFISH** (*Abudefduf caeruleus*): an extremely active little Pacific marine fish whose intense, minerallike blue coloration makes it a handsome, if pugnacious, addition to saltwater community aquaria. An unusual camouflage feature is the fish's ability to lose its color at will, as though a strong bleach suddenly had been added to the water. *Habitat:* Indo-Pacific waters. *Diet:* Varied. NOTE: Small single specimens are recommended for community tanks, but even they should not be mixed with such delicately-finned species as the BLUE REEF FISH (*Chromis marginatus*).

BLUE GOURAMI (*Trichogaster trichopterus*): One of the most popular of all freshwater fishes, this sizable silver-blue creature is marked with two small spots on each side, one in the center of its body and the other at the base of the tail. It behaves well in commu-

nity tanks, except with very small fishes, breeds readily, spawns prolifically, and grows well in large tanks. *Habitat:* Sumatra. *Diet:* Extremely varied, with most standard aquarium foods accepted.

BLUE GULARIS (*Aphyosemion coeruleum*): This good-sized, extremely colorful and vividly marked killie is generally unpopular among aquarists. It is aggressive, tends to refuse any but live foods, and is reluctant to breed in captivity. *Habitat:* West Africa. *Diet:* Small live fish in generous quantities and, depending on the habits of the individual specimen, chunks of earthworm, beef heart.

BLUE PANCHAX (*Aplocheilus panchax*): Although not very colorful, this medium-sized fish gets along well with other species its own size or larger and breeds readily. *Habitat:* Southeast Asia, Malay Peninsula, India, Burma. *Diet:* Varied, with small live foods preferred.

BLUE PETROTILAPIA (*Petrotilapia tridentiger*): a colorful, medium-sized mouthbreeder with a preference for slightly brackish water. It is too bellicose to be kept in community tanks. *Habitat:* Malawi Lake (Nyasa), Africa. *Diet:* Live foods, herbaceous matter.

BLUE REEF FISH (*Chromis marginatus*): This good-sized, brilliantly irridescent, gracefully shaped marine fish is rather shy by nature and needs plenty of well-aerated water. Its very delicate fins are extremely vulnerable to the depredations of such nippers as the BLUE DEMOISELLE (*Abudefduf caeruleus*), from which it should be kept well separated. *Habitat:* Indo-Pacific waters. *Diet:* Fish roe, chopped earthworms, shrimp, small live foods.

BLUE TANG: *see* YELLOW TANG.

BOLIVIAN SUCKER CATFISH (*Plecostomus bolivianus*): Its sharp, spiny fins make this a difficult fish to handle, but it is a useful, peaceable inhabitant of community tanks, which it keeps free of algae. Easily distinguishable by its disproportionately large dorsal fin with its rows of dark spots. *Habitat:* Bolivia. *Diet:* Live and frozen foods, herbaceous matter.

BOWFIN or **MUDFISH** or **DOGFISH** (*Amia calva*): This very large, rather primitive creature is not a true tropical fish, but is kept as a curiosity by some hobbyists. Although easily tamed, it is a voracious predator and should not be kept in a community tank. Distinguishable by its long, rippling dorsal fin, a horizontal line that passes through its eye, and a false eyespot at the base of its tail. *Habitat:* Much of the eastern half of the United States. *Diet:* Live foods.

BREDER'S BETTA (*Betta brederi*): This dowdier relative of the BETTA , or Siamese fighting fish, is yellow-brown with blue highlights on its scales. It lacks the spectacular fin development of *Betta splendens*. Best kept in isolation from other species, it is a mouthbreeder and goes through an elaborate spawning ritual. *Habitat:* Java, Sumatra. *Diet:* Live foods.

BREEDING TROPICAL FISH: In circumstances that are at least minimally propitious, most freshwater tropical fish will propagate their kind in captivity. By and large, the easiest fish to breed are the live-bearers, which almost unfailingly will initiate a courtship ritual, even in the most discouraging of

Bowfin

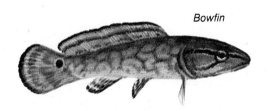

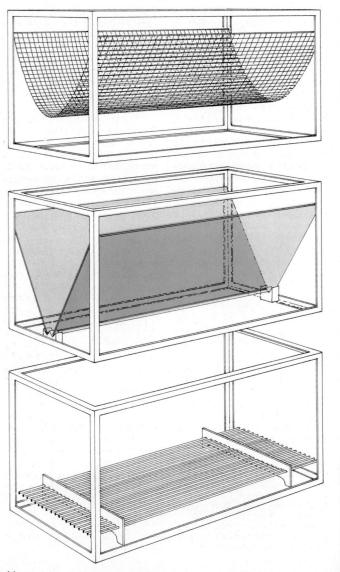

44

situations. Since male live-bearers are almost indefatigable, however, two or more females should be alloted to each fertile male. Live-bearers, like most other fish, tend to cannibalize their young if given the opportunity to do so. Newly hatched fry, therefore, should either be completely isolated from their parents (and, needless to say, other predators) or provided with cover—usually in the form of a dense concentration of floating plants—adequate for their protection. Isolation is most easily accomplished by means of a variety of breeding traps: slotted or mesh-covered compartments, the apertures of which permit the fry, but not the adults, to pass.

Although the various members of the family Cyprinodontidae, the egg-laying tooth carps, do not breed as readily as the live-bearers, most known species have propagated in captivity in favorable circumstances. The egg-hangers, for example, usually require water of a softness under 50 ppm CaCo3 (*see* WATER) and a device known as a breeding mop, which simulates a floating plant by providing hanging cover for the fry and which should be installed in a dark corner of the aquarium. One such mop (usually made of nylon wool strings attached to a cork) usually is suffi-

cient for a healthy male and three females that, in the course of a week, may lay 250 eggs among them. Once the eggs are laid, the mop should be removed from the tank with some of the tank water and maintained at a temperature of 68 to 73° F. Hatching usually occurs within 14 to 24 days.

The egg-buriers are made up of the various so-called "annual fishes," which is to say, species native to locales that undergo a pronounced dry season during which ponds and water holes dry up completely and the adult generation dies off. Before succumbing, however, the egg-buriers spawn in the mud bottoms of their habitats, and their eggs remain dormant until the onset of the rainy season activates them. In captivity, the egg-buriers can be induced to breed by teaming a male with three females after lining the tank bottom with a layer of peat. Once they have paired off, the male and his female choice of the moment will repeatedly dive down into the peat, where the female deposits her eggs. After a week or ten days (at which point the females have earned a well-deserved rest), the peat should be filtered through a cloth or net with a mesh fine enough to keep the eggs from passing through it. The eggs thus preserved then should be stored in a plastic container and allowed to become partially dry over a period of several days. The container is covered and incubated for about four months at 68 to 70° F. Finally, soft acid water is added, after which the eggs hatch out in a matter of hours.

OPPOSITE: *Three common types of breeding traps used by professional and home aquarists. The plastic mesh device (top), open-bottomed glass or plastic V (center), and closely spaced rod arrangement (bottom) all serve to isolate parents from their fry.*

45

Breeding Tropical Fish

—Tank Furnishings

Tuft of fibre or mop, round pebbles, for egg scatterers, as Barbs, Danios, etc.

Nylon mop and peat base, for scatterers like Characin

Floating mop for egg hangers, peat base for bottom spawners

Floating fern for nest builders

Flat-topped stone, lime-free gravel for egg placers

The egg-scatterers, mostly characins and carps, deposit their eggs in a nu... be assigned ... eral categori... are adhesiv... eggs are n... that lay adh... provided with... scattered thi... finely divide... in question i... leaping egg...

JUMPING ... *arnoldi*), the ... aquarium sh... ject severa... waterline, w... deposited. ... adhesive eg... with conside... ferably in th... plants bea... leaves.

Although ... that hybrid ...

chiefly among oviviparous species, many of the more spectacular hybridizations have involved the domesticated goldfish (*Carassius auratus*) and its various offshoots. In any event, cross-fertilization is possible only between closely related species, and when distantly related species do manage to mate, the offspring usually are sterile, physically defective, or

otherwise unsuited to continue the line. Within a given genus, how-ever, the chances for successful hybridization are much greater, with the real most frequent inci-dence of success occurring bet... ... the raising of powder blue ... ... ively a hit-or-miss affair; ... ...ces far more prevalent than ... ... The existing literature on the ...

Congo. *Diet:* Live foods.

BRILLIANT RASBORA or **EINTHOVEN'S RASBORA** (*Rasbora einthoveni*): an attractive, iridescent, hyperactive fish with a dark stripe running from snout to tail. It is displayed to best advantage in schools and under strong natural light. *Habitat:* Southeast Asia, Malay Archipelago. *Diet:* Varied.

Brilliant Rasbora

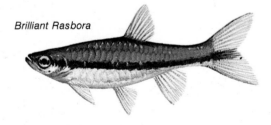

Bumblebeefish

BRINE SHRIMP (*Artemia salina*): a diminutive crustacean normally found in heavily saline waters and used extensively as tropical fish food. The great advantages of brine shrimp over other small live foods are their cleanliness, the ease with which they can be transported and stored before they have hatched, and the almost indefinite viability of their powdery roe so long as it is kept in a state of dry dormancy. *Habitat:* Great Salt Lake, Utah, California coastal waters, and elsewhere. *Diet:* Algae, baker's yeast.

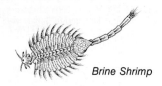

Brine Shrimp

BRISTLE-NOSE: any of several members of family Loricariidae equipped with a number of bristlelike sensors; most notably *Ancistrus lineolatus*, a good-sized nocturnal catfish with dark mottlings on a bluish body. *Habitat:* Upper Amazon River. *Diet:* Highly varied, with small live foods, herbaceous matter, and tank detritus.

preferred. NOTE: Needs dark hiding places.

BROAD-SOLE: *see* SOLE.

BRONZE CATFISH: *see* AENEUS CATFISH.

BUBBLE-NEST BUILDERS: any of various members of the family ANABANTIDAE that typically spawn in a nest of floating bubbles constructed by the male, who secretes a viscous salivary "glue" for the purpose. The BETTA (*Betta splendens*) is a typical bubble-nest builder.

BUMBLEBEEFISH (*Brachygobius xanthozona*): This extremely attractive little goby takes its name from the striking resemblance of its markings, size, demeanor, and movements to those of the common honeybees. Yellow or yellow-orange with four black vertical bands that completely encircle its body, the fish is short-finned and spends much of its time hovering in a convincingly beelike fashion that many observers find rather humorous. Somewhat fragile, they do not adapt well to community tanks and required sheltering hiding places in slightly brackish water. *Habitat:* Borneo, Sumatra, Java. *Diet:* Small live foods.

BUNOCEPHALIDAE: the taxonomic family comprising several

similar species of broad-headed South American catfishes with slender, tapering, elongated bodies.

BURMESE BADIS (*Badis badis burmanicus*): a small, extremely shy nandid. It is interestingly marked with alternating red and blue spots arranged in neat rows on a silver-gray ground. A row of darker spots runs along the base of the dorsal fin. Unhappy in community aquaria. *Habitat:* Burma. *Diet:* Small live foods.

BUSHY-MOUTHED CATFISH (*Xenocara dolichoptera*): This blue-black armored catfish resembles the somewhat larger *Ancistrus lineolatus* (*see* BRISTLE-NOSE), both physically and in its habits. Given a good hiding place in a community tank, it will spawn readily. *Habitat:* Northeastern Brazil. *Diet:* Omniverous.

BUTTER HAMLET (*Hypoplectrus unicolor*): One of the commonest of the West Indian marine aquarium fishes, this is a small yellow-gray creature that bears blue markings on its head and a black disc at the caudal base. *Habitat:* Florida coastal waters, West Indies. *Diet:* Coarsely chopped shrimp, live earthworms, small minnows, all made clearly visible to the fish.

BUTTERFLY FISH: (1) Any of several marine fishes, including the BANDED B.F. (*Chaetodon striatus*), FOUR-EYED B.F. (*Chaetodon capistratus*), and LONG-FINNED B.F. (*Heniochus acuminatus*). (2) *Pantadon buchholzi*, a freshwater "flying" species unique to the genus *Pantadon* and distinguished by its winglike pectoral fins and capacious, obliquely positioned mouth. *Habitat:* Equatorial West Africa. *Diet:* Live

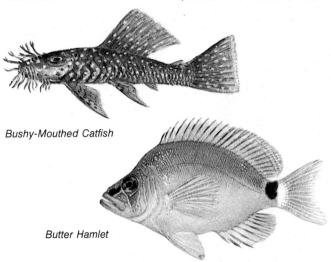

Bushy-Mouthed Catfish

Butter Hamlet

Butterfly Mudskipper

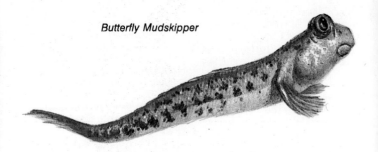

flying insects, other live insects, and (less preferable) minced shrimp.

BUTTERFLY MUDSKIPPER (*Periophthalmus papilio*): This good-sized, highly unusual amphibious fish is distinguishable by its froglike head and markings, protuberant eyes, and limblike pectoral fins. Easily tamed and fond of slightly brackish water, it must be isolated from other species. *Habitat:* West African littoral from Dakar almost to the Tropic of Cancer and for a considerable distance inland. *Diet:* Varied, with larger foods and live flying insects preferred.

CALLICHTHYDAE: the taxonomic family consisting of various so-called smooth armored catfishes, all native to South America and all encased in a series of overlapping bony plates. The CASCUDO (*Hoplosternum littorale*) and AENEUS CATFISH (*Corydoras aeneus*) are typical species.

CALLIONYMIDAE: the taxonomic family comprising the various dragonets, relatively little-known Pacific marine fishes, of which most genera characteristically possess two dorsal fins.

CALLISTUS TETRA or **SERPA TETRA** (*Hyphessobrycon callistus callistus*): This small, well-behaved red tetra bears a black spot on its dorsal fin and a vertical black mark which crosses the horizontal line near the gill cover. Best kept in small schools and in well-planted tanks. *Habitat:* Paraguay and the neighboring portion of Brazil. *Diet:* Varied.

CANTHIGASTERIDAE: the taxonomic family made up of the so-called sharp-nosed puffers, small, narrow-snouted marine blowfishes most commonly found around tropical Pacific reefs.

CARDINAL FISH (*Apogon maculatus*): Nocturnally active, this brilliant red marine fish has a gold stripe running through its eye. Somewhat aggressive and endowed with a good appetite, it should not be kept in community aquaria with species smaller than itself and requires dark hiding places. *Habitat:* Western Atlantic waters. *Diet:* Live earthworms, coarsely chopped shrimp.

Cardinal Fish

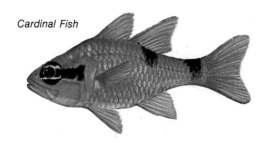

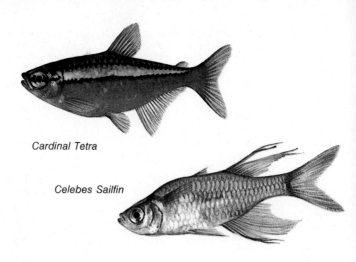

Cardinal Tetra

Celebes Sailfin

CARDINAL TETRA (*Cheirodon axelrodi*): Although similar to the neon tetra, this small, striking characin's red coloration is more vivid and more extensive, extending onto the lower head It should be kept in schools, both for its own happiness and for maximum aesthetic satisfaction. *Habitat:* Rio Negro, Brazil. *Diet:* Varied small foods.

CARP: (1) (*Cyprinus carpio*) an omniverous freshwater food fish of Asiatic origin, now widely distributed throughout the temperate regions. Small young specimens frequently are introduced into hobbyists' aquaria, where they act as effective, if somewhat disruptive, scavengers. (2) Any of numerous members of the family Cyprinidae, the largest family of fishes known, including the various minnows, goldfishes, barbs, danios, rasboras.

CASCUDO or **HOPLO** (*Hoplosternum littorale*): a large, peaceful catfish that spawns by depositing its eggs on the undersides of floating objects. *Habitat:* Much of South America and Trinidad. *Diet:* Varied, with brine shrimp, tubifex worms, and scavenged material preferred.

CATFISH: any of numerous scaleless, largely freshwater fishes assigned to the order Siluriformes and usually bearing barbels, or "whiskers," on their upper jaws.

The Aeneus Catfish is a popular breed

CELEBES SAILFIN or **CELEBES RAINBOW FISH** (*Telmatherina ladigesi*): a handsome, medium-sized silvery fish with large, graceful lemon-yellow dorsal and anal fins (black-edged in the males). *Habitat:* Celebes. *Diet:* Varied. NOTE: Prefers sunlight and slightly saline water.

CELESTIAL GOLDFISH: a variety of *Carassius auratus* (*see* GOLDFISH) similar to the eggfish, but with protuberant globular eyes.

CENTRARCHIDAE: the taxonomic family comprising the North American sunfishes and black basses, characterized by two nostrils on each side of the head.

CENTRISCIDAE: the taxonomic family comprising the shrimp-fishes, small marine creatures that swim head-down and are charac-terized by attenuated snouts and a streamlined, knife-like silhouette. Well-suited to community aquaria, they thrive best in schools.

CEYLON PANCHAX or **DAY'S PANCHAX** (*Aplocheilus dayi*): a medium-sized olive-green killie formerly known as *Panchax panchax*. A peaceable creature if kept with fish its own size or larger, it is easily bred in tanks rich in surface plant life. *Habitat:* India, Malay Peninsula, Sri Lanka. *Diet:* Varied, small live foods preferred.

CEYLONESE FIRE BARB (*Rasbora vaterifloris*): An attractive little purple-and-orange creature, it spawns readily but, if left to its own devices, will cannibalize its eggs. It is extremely active and it needs plenty of room. *Habitat:* Sri Lanka. *Diet:* Varied, with small live foods preferred.

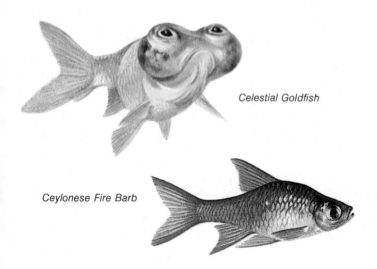

Celestial Goldfish

Ceylonese Fire Barb

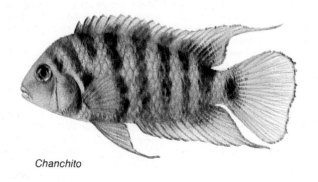

Chanchito

CHAETODONOTIDAE: the taxonomic family embracing the various marine reef fishes commonly called "BUTTERFLY FISHES," and generally prized for their brilliant color, stately carriage, and relatively small size.

CHANCHITO or **CHANCHITA** (*Cichlasoma facetum*): Hardy, good-sized, and easily bred, this dark-banded greenish fish is reputed to be the first cichlid to be domesticated (in 1884). Peaceable according to some authorities and pugnacious according to others, it is in any event too large, at 7 or 8 inches, for most community aquaria. *Habitat:* Southern Brazil and northern Argentina. *Diet:* Varied, with meaty foods preferred. NOTE: Lives well outdoors in temperatures above 60° F.

CHANDIDAE: Native to the estuaries and shallows of the Indian Ocean and the western Pacific, most chandids are translucent and bear two connected dorsal fins, of which one is spiny. The GLASSFISH (*Chanda lala*) is a typical species.

CHANNIDAE: the taxonomic family of so-called snakeheads—various air-breathing species distinguishable by their elongated bodies, spineless fins, and enormous appetites.

CHARACIDAE: Together with the carps and catfishes, the family Characidae, or characins, belong to the taxonomic order Ostariophysi and comprise one of the largest known families of fishes. Widely distributed throughout Central and South America and tropical Africa, the Characidae generally are distinguishable from the Cyprinidae, which they tend closely to resemble, by their toothed jaws and adipose fins. The various tetras, piranhas, pencil-fishes belong to the family.

CHECKERBOARD CICHLID (*Crenicara maculata*): A small, attractive species usually characterized as a dwarf cichlid, it has a yellowish body marked with two rows of staggered dark spots and (in the male) blue and yellow-orange streaks in the ventral fins. Difficult to breed and somewhat fragile. *Habitat:* Central and lower Amazon region. *Diet:* Varied, with individual specimens developing individual preferences.

CHECKERED BARB or **CHECKER BARB** (*Capoeta oligolepis*): a small, attractive, and easily bred fish. The males take on heightened color during breeding, at which time they become an iridescent red-orange with purple accents. *Habitat:* Sumatra. *Diet:* Varied.

CHERRY BARB (*Capoeta titteya*): As is the case with the checkered barb, the male of this very popular species is most resplendent during breeding, when its color is a deep cherry-red. Cherry barbs are easily bred, but the parents tend to cannibalize their eggs which should be given adequate plant cover. *Habitat:* Sri Lanka. *Diet:* Varied, with brine shrimp preferred.

CHERUBFISH (*Centropyge argi*): a small spade-shaped marine butterfly fish with a purplish body and yellow-orange head. Because members of the species are extremely pugnacious toward each other, they should be provided with accessible hiding places. *Habitat:* Indo-Pacific waters. *Diet:* Brine shrimp and finely chopped foods.

CHILL: *see* DISEASES OF TROPICAL FISH.

CHINESE ALGAE-EATER (*Gyrinocheilus aymonieri*): a medium-sized fish equipped with a sucking-disc that enables it to anchor itself on the bottoms of swift, shallow streams. As its name implies, it will keep aquaria free of green algae. *Habitat* (its popular name notwithstanding): Thailand. *Diet:* Strictly herbaceous, with

Cherubfish

Chocolate Gourami

Cinnamon Killie

crushed leaf vegetables appropriate in lieu of algae.

CHOCOLATE GOURAMI (*Sphaerichthys osphromenoides*): a small, quite handsome chocolate-brown species of gourami marked with mottled vertical bands. Its breeding habits are the subject of considerable controversy. Best kept with its own kind and in slightly acid, quite warm water. *Habitat:* Malaya, Sumatra. *Diet:* Small live foods.

CICHLIDAE: the taxonomic family comprising the cichlids, a group of mostly large, spiny-rayed fishes bearing a single nostril on each side of the head. They tend to be combative among themselves and, during courtship and spawning, toward other species. Characteristically rather flat of body and with slightly prognathous lower jaws and small, sharp teeth, the family is indigenous chiefly to the Americas and Africa and includes such species as the Jack Dempsey (*Cichlasoma biocellatum*), oscar (*Astronotus oscellatus*), firemouth (*Cichlasoma meeki*), orange chromide (*Etroplus maculatus*), and jewel cichlid (*Hemichromis bimaculatus*).

CINNAMON KILLIE (*Aphyosemion cinnamomeum*): a very handsome, rather small fish that takes its name from its red-brown body coloration. Its caudal, anal, and ventral fins are yellow-edged and its dorsal fin spotted and edged with blue. Not adaptable to community tanks. *Habitat:* Equatorial West Africa. *Diet:* Small live or frozen foods.

CIRRHITIDAE: the taxonomic family embracing the various marine hawkfishes, related to the Indo-Pacific scorpion fishes.

CLASSIFICATION OF FISH: All the world's fishes belong to the phylum Chordata, that is, the spined animals, and the taxonomic superclass Pisces, which comprises one class (Placodermi) of extinct armored fishes, and three classes of extant fishes: Agnatha, the jawless fishes; Chondrichthyes, the cartilaginous sharks and rays; and Osteichthyses, the bony fishes. With very few exceptions, it is to the latter group that the tropical aquarium fish belong. Moving progressively from the general toward the particular, the classes are divided into orders, suborders, and families before being broken down further into genera and species. For all practical purposes, the home aquarist's largest area of concern is the family, for genera of the same family tend to live in similar environments and follow similar breeding patterns, while the differences between the various species of any genera are often negligible and sometimes not very readily discernible. With a general knowledge of the various families and their distinguishing characteristics at his command, the tropical fish enthusiast is not likely to be at a complete loss, even when faced with a species unknown to him.

Like most organisms known to man, tropical fish have both a scientific and a popular name. Unlike most branches of zoology, however, the study of tropical fish is largely a concern of laymen—often laymen contending for recognition as discoverers of previously unknown species—and, consequently, considerable nomenclatural confusion plagues the literature, with near-chaos the prevailing condition where popular names are concerned. Because most aquarists *are* laymen, this book gives precedence to popular names, simply because "Jack Dempsey" is somewhat more memorable, at least to nonlatinists, than "*Cichlasoma biocellatum*." It would be good policy, nonetheless, for serious hobbyists to familiarize themselves with at least the rudiments of scientific nomenclature in the interest of precision. A descriptive popular name may easily be given to a half-dozen or so species and a single species may bear two Latin names while scientists in disagreement argue their cases. No two species, though, are likely to be given a single Latin name, and Latin terminology, once it is understood, is a good deal more informative than popular nomenclature. *Abromites microcephalus*, for example, at least tells us that the fish in question resembles a bream and has a small head. The same fish's common name, Norman's headstander, tells us very little, for there are numerous headstanders belonging to the family Characidae —and quite a few Normans belonging to the genus *Homo* and the family Hominidae.

OVERLEAF: *Schematic diagrams showing taxonomic classification of fauna (left) and aquatic vertebrates (right). The latter are narrowed down to genera here, but stop short of particular species of fish.*

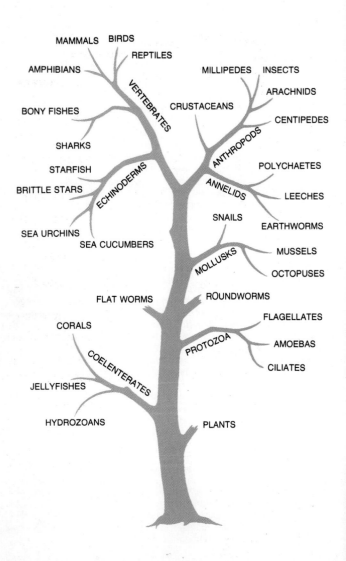

MAMMALS BIRDS
REPTILES
AMPHIBIANS
VERTEBRATES
BONY FISHES
SHARKS
STARFISH
BRITTLE STARS
ECHINODERMS
SEA URCHINS
SEA CUCUMBERS

MILLIPEDES INSECTS
ARACHNIDS
CRUSTACEANS
CENTIPEDES
ANTHROPODS
POLYCHAETES
ANNELIDS
LEECHES
SNAILS
EARTHWORMS
MUSSELS
MOLLUSKS
OCTOPUSES
FLAT WORMS ROUNDWORMS
FLAGELLATES
CORALS
PROTOZOA AMOEBAS
COELENTERATES
CILIATES
JELLYFISHES
HYDROZOANS PLANTS

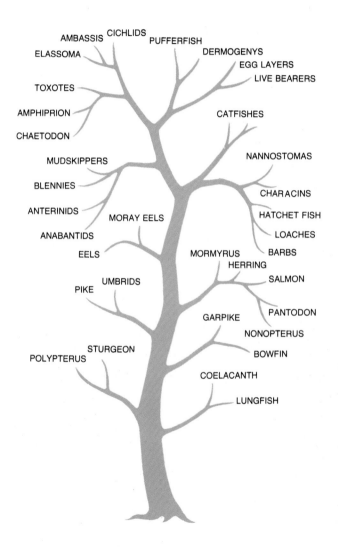

AMBASSIS CICHLIDS PUFFERFISH
ELASSOMA DERMOGENYS
EGG LAYERS
LIVE BEARERS
TOXOTES
AMPHIPRION CATFISHES
CHAETODON
NANNOSTOMAS
MUDSKIPPERS
BLENNIES CHARACINS
ANTERINIDS HATCHET FISH
MORAY EELS LOACHES
ANABANTIDS BARBS
EELS MORMYRUS HERRING
UMBRIDS SALMON
PIKE PANTODON
GARPIKE NONOPTERUS
STURGEON BOWFIN
POLYPTERUS COELACANTH
LUNGFISH

59

Climbing Perch

CLIMBING PERCH (*Anabas testudineus*): In its natural habitat this gray-green labyrinth fish (*see* ANABANTIDAE) can propel itself over dry land for several hundred yards at a stretch by "walking" on its pectoral fins. It attains a length of 10 inches or more in the wild and is commonly used as a food fish in Asia. Not a good mixer, the species should be kept to itself. *Habitat:* Widely distributed throughout southern China, Southeast Asia, the Phillippines, and the Malay Archipelago. *Diet:* Widely varied, with meaty foods preferred.

CLINIDAE: *see* BLENNIIDAE.

CLOWN ANEMONE or **ANEMONE FISH** (*Amphiprion percula* or *A. sebae*): a small, hardy, vividly marked marine fish very popular for its alternating orange and white markings and its rather humorous aspect. It is much given to hiding among the tentacles of various toxic anemones, to whose poisons it is immune and for which it provides food and grooming. *Habitat:* Indian Ocean and the coastal waters of Southeast Asia. *Diet:* Dry foods, chopped shrimp and worms, brine shrimp.

CLOWN BARB (*Barbodes everetti*): This relatively good-sized, handsomely marked fish is distinguishable by its deep red fins and the clearly defined blue-black markings on its sides. A prolific breeder and a hearty feeder, it is destructive of plants and smaller fish, but quite popular nonetheless. *Habitat:* Maylay Peninsula, Borneo. *Diet:* Omnivorous.

CLOWN KILLIE (*Epiplatys annulatus*): This quite small and rather rare fish is handsomely marked with alternating brown and yellow bands and vivid blues and reds in the anal, dorsal, and caudal fins. Too small and water-sensitive for most community tanks. *Habitat:* West Africa. *Diet:* Most small live aquarium foods.

CLOWN LOACH or **TIGER BOTIA** (*Botia macracantha*): A durable, popular, active creature, it has a red-finned orange body clearly marked with three black vertical bands. Somewhat larger and less nocturnal than most loaches, it is peaceful and an active scavenger. *Habitat:* Borneo and its vicinity. *Diet:* Small live foods, aquarium detritus.

CLOWN TRIGGERFISH (*Balistoides niger*): Resembling a living painting by Miro, this spectacular mutlicolored creature is large, relatively rare, quite expensive, and like most marine triggerfishes, easily trained to perform various tricks. *Habitat:* Tropical Indo-Pacific region. *Diet:* Chopped shrimp, earthworms and similar coarse, meaty foods, unwanted small aquarium fish.

COBITIDAE: the taxonomic family comprising the loaches, none of which are found in the New World and all of which have at least three pairs of barbels growing on or near the snout. Although most loaches are eellike in shape, the clown, or tiger, loach (*Botia macracantha*) is an exception.

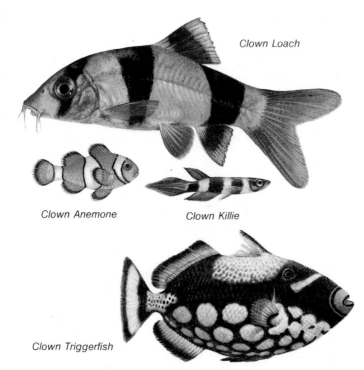

Clown Loach

Clown Anemone

Clown Killie

Clown Triggerfish

COBRA FISH: see LIONFISH.

COCHU'S CATFISH (*Corydoras cochui*): One of the smallest of the various *Corydoras* species, this irregularly marked gray-brown fish is well suited to life in community aquaria. *Habitat:* Brazil. *Diet:* Any small foods, tank detritus.

COLUMNARIS: see DISEASES OF TROPICAL FISH.

COMB-TAIL PARADISE FISH or **COMB-TAIL** (*Belontia signata*): Similar to the paradise fish (*Macropodus opercularis*), this reddish-brown labyrinth fish (family ANABANTIDAE) is characterized by the attenuated filaments on its dorsal and caudal fins. Voracious and bellicose toward smaller fishes, it has been known to cannibalize its young. *Habitat:* Sri Lanka. *Diet:* Varied, with meaty foods preferred.

COMET GOLDFISH: a fancy variety of *Carassius auratus* (see GOLDFISH) distinguished by its extensive fin development, especially its graceful, flowing tail.

COMMON PUFFER-FISH or **MAYLAYAN PUFFER** (*Tetraodon cutcutia*): One of the best-known members of the family Tetraodontidae, or blowfishes, this sizable, clearly spotted native of brackish waters swims with a hovering motion and inflates itself like a balloon when threatened with danger or removed from the water.

Comb-Tail Paradise Fish

Comet Goldfish

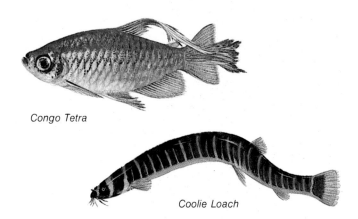

Congo Tetra

Coolie Loach

Although popular and easily tamed, it should not be introduced into community tanks. *Habitat:* India, Malay Peninsula. *Diet:* Larger live foods, coarsely chopped shrimp, unwanted live snails. NOTE: Should be kept in slightly salt water.

COMPOSTS: *see* AQUARIUM CARE AND MANAGEMENT.

CONGO PUFFER (*Tetraodon miurus*): a curious freshwater blowfish whose color changes to match its surroundings and whose uptilted jaws are enormously powerful. It should not be kept in community tanks. *Habitat:* Congo. *Diet:* Chopped earthworms, adult brine shrimp, unwanted live fish, live snails.

CONGO TETRA or **FEATHERTAIL TETRA** (*Micralestes interruptus* or *Phenacogrammus i.*): A sizable characin with large iridescent scales and white-edged violet fins, it is distinguished by the characteristic feathery extension that projects from the tail, giving the entire caudal fin the appearance of an arrowhead. *Habitat:* Congo. *Diet:* Live, frozen and coarsely chopped meaty foods.

CONGRIDAE: the taxonomic family embracing the marine conger eels, distinguishable from the moray eels (family MURAENIDAE) by their pectoral fins.

CONVICT CICHLID or **ZEBRA CICHLID** (*Cichlasoma nigrofasciatum*): This handsomely striped cichlid is at its best when young, before the distinctive black bands for which it is named begin to fade. Body color varies from one specimen to another, with most either silvery or purplish on the sides and with yellow backs. *Habitat:* Central America. *Diet:* Varied, with chopped beef heart preferred.

COOLIE (or **KUHLII**) **LOACH** (*Acanthopthalmus kuhlii*): This very popular scavenger is known for its elongated, brown-banded yellowish body and its ability to enter and remove food from crevices and openings inaccessible to

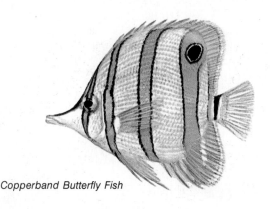

Copperband Butterfly Fish

other species. Largely nocturnal, it behaves well in community tanks. *Habitat:* Northeastern India, Burma, Malay Archipelago. *Diet:* Small live foods, tankmates' leftovers.

COPPERBAND BUTTERFLY FISH or **LONGNOSE AUSTRALIAN BUTTERFLY** (*Chelmon rostratus*): This spectacularly marked marine fish bears three narrow, copper-orange vertical bands, all of them edged in black and one running through the eye, on its gleaming silver sides. There is a broader, less clearly defined area the same color near the base of the caudal fin, the upper portion of which area is marked with a precisely outlined ocellus. The fish's small mouth and long, tubular oral cavity prevent it from eating any but the smallest of foods. *Habitat:* Indo-Pacific region. *Diet:* Tubifex worms, small brine shrimp.

CORAL: (1) Any of various marine compound polyps having calcareous skeletons, (2) the individual skeletons of any of these creatures, or (3) the collective skeletons of myriad members of one such species, fused to produce a stony mass that may range in magnitude from a small plantlike shape to an entire island or reef. Used primarily for decoration by saltwater aquarists, coral also provides suitable hiding places for those fish that tend to be shy. All coral, whether obtained commercially or collected from the sea, should be thoroughly cleaned (first with fresh water, then in a chlorinated disinfectant and again in fresh water, and then bleached in sunlight) before being introduced into the aquarium.

In general, it is inadvisable to introduce corals into freshwater aquaria or among species that do not normally encounter them in their natural habitats.

A colony of fire or stinging coral below Elkhorn coral on a platform reef in the Florida keys.

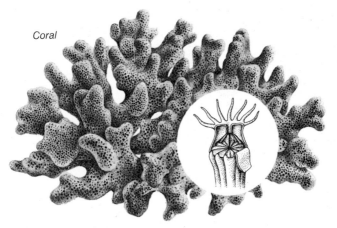

A typical coral formation, with a single organism shown in inset.

Croaking Tetra

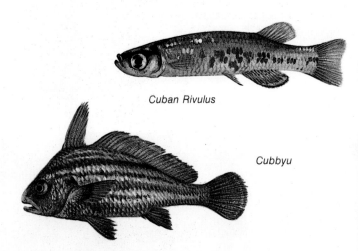

Cuban Rivulus

Cubbyu

CROAKING GOURAMI (*Ctenops vittatus* or *Trichopsis v.*): This small, indistinctly striped blue-gray fish is more readily recognized by its striking blue eyes than by the faint croaking sound it emits when spawning. *Habitat:* Southeast Asia, Malay Archipelago. *Diet:* Varied, with small live foods preferred. NOTE: Requires water heated to 82°-85° F.

CROAKING TETRA (*Mimagoniates inequalis*): Very well-behaved, this brown-backed, silver-sided fish breathes at the surface and exhales underwater, producing a faint croaking sound. *Habitat:* Southeastern Brazil. *Diet:* Varied.

CRUSTACEAN: any of numerous freshwater and marine arthropods, including the shrimps, crayfishes, lobsters, crabs, and water fleas, protected by a hard, often articulated, covering.

CUBAN RIVULUS (*Rivulus cylindraceus*): Some 2½ inches long, the female of the species is slightly larger than the male and, unlike her mate, bears an ocellus (eye spot) on her brown body at the upper base of the caudal fin. Easily bred and well behaved in community tanks. *Habitat:* Cuba. *Diet:* Small live foods.

CUBBYU or **HIGH HAT** (*Equetus acuminatus*): This small, rather delicate marine fish is vividly marked with a series of broken black-and-white stripes running the length of its body. It tends to be shy and is quite vulnerable to the depredations of demoiselles and similar fin-nippers. Best kept exclusively with its own kind. *Habitat:* Florida, West Indies. *Diet:* Brine shrimp, small worms and minnows, finely chopped shrimp.

CYPRINIDAE: the taxonomic family comprising some 1,500 species of carp or carplike fish, including the various forms of the goldfish (*Carassius auratus*), the minnows, barbs, rasboras, and danios.

CYPRINODONTIDAE: the taxonomic family made up of the various so-called egg-laying tooth carps or killifish, which include the EGG-BURIERS, EGG-HANGERS, and egg-scatterers.

D

DADIO (*Laubuca dadiburjori*): Small, easily kept, and quite active, this yellow-green fish bears a gold-edged blue stripe that extends from the gill cover area to the base of the caudal fin. It is a lively jumper and requires a covered tank. *Habitat:* Western India. *Diet:* Varied, with no discernible preferences.

DAMSELFISH or **DEMOISELLE:** *see* ANEMONE FISH.

DANIO: any of several members of the family Cyprinidae, usually small, minnowlike, and bearing a pair of barbels on the snout, *e.g.*, the popular zebra danio (*Brachydanio rerio*), pearl danio (*B. albolineatus*), giant danio (*B. malabaricus*), and spotted danio (*B. nigrofasciatus*).

DAPHNIA (*plural:* **DAPHNIAE**): any of several minute freshwater crustaceans of the genus *Daphnia*, much used live, dried, or frozen as food for tropical fish. Daphniae have laxative properties and therefore a diet in which they appear in significant numbers should be augmented with one or more starchy foods.

DAVID'S UPSIDE-DOWN CATFISH (*Synodontis davidi*): Like its larger cousin *Synodontis nigriventris*, this small, mottled brown catfish swims belly-up. Well-

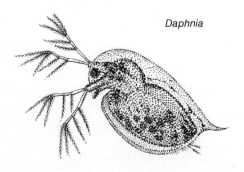

Daphnia

behaved in community tanks, it is seminocturnal and requires hiding places. *Habitat:* Stanley Pool, Africa. *Diet:* Varied, with some herbaceous matter included.

DAY'S PANCHAX: *see* CEYLON PANCHAX.

DAY'S PARADISE FISH (*Macropodus cupanus dayi* or *Polyacanthus dayi*): A small brown anabantid, its body is marked with two horizontal stripes and its anal and caudal fins are edged in blue. It is hardy and peaceable, but its jumping propensities make a covered tank obligatory. *Habitat:* Eastern India, western Burma, Sri Lanka. *Diet:* Varied.

DEMON FISH or **JURUPARI** or **EARTHEATER** (*Geophagus jurupari*): a good-sized, blue-dotted, big-eyed cichlid with an unusually long, sloping forehead. It is quite peaceable despite its most popular common name and incubates its young in its mouth. *Habitat:* Northeast coast of South America. *Diet:* Dry and small live foods.

DIAMOND SUNFISH (*Enneacanthus gloriosus*): Not a true tropical fish but popular with aquarists, this is an extremely attractive little creature bearing a liberal speckling of blue dots on a brown ground. It behaves well in community tanks but requires colder water than most tropical fish find comfortable. *Habitat:* East coast of the United States as far north as New York state. *Diet:* Varied, with small live or frozen foods preferred.

DIAMOND TETRA (*Moekhausia pittieri*): Bearing a prominent crested dorsal fin and an unusually large anal fin, this silver-blue, red-

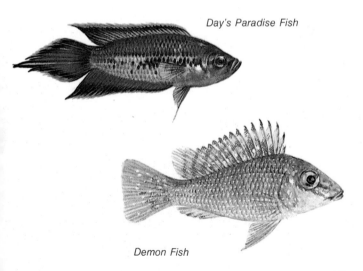

Day's Paradise Fish

Demon Fish

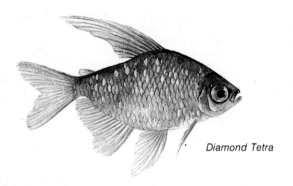
Diamond Tetra

eyed species is one of the most striking of the characins. Small, peaceful, and quite active, it makes a welcome addition to community aquaria. *Habitat:* Venezuela. *Diet:* Extremely varied, with some herbaceous matter recommended.

DIMIDIATUS (*Nannochromis dimidiatus*): Easily spawned and well-behaved in community tanks, this is a medium-sized purplish species in which the smaller female's throat is marked with a blue-green "glow." *Habitat:* Congo. *Diet:* Live foods.

DIODONTIDAE: the taxonomic family comprising the various porcupine fish or marine puffers, characterized by the sharp erectile spines that cover most of their bodies and serve as a defence mechanism when the imperiled fish inflates itself.

DISCUS: *see* RED DISCUS.

DISEASES OF TROPICAL FISH: Like all other fauna, aquarium fish are subject to illness, injury, disease, and debilitation. Unfortunately, however, few veterinarians

are any better equipped to treat aquatic patients than are most laymen. Consequently, home aquarists must cope as best they can with the ailments of their pets. To this end, it is worth remembering that here, as elsewhere, prevention is more desirable than cure, and that for the most part prevention takes the form of a few obvious precautions:

1. Proper aquarium hygiene should be maintained at all times, with aquaria adequately filtered and aerated, kept at suitable temperatures, and kept free of accumulated wastes and uneaten food.

2. All newly acquired fish should be quarantined in a separate tank until all danger of transmission of infectious disease or parasites is past.

3. Tropical fish should never be subjected to abrupt changes of water temperature.

4. Aquaria should never be overcrowded.

5. Naturally hostile and naturally vulnerable fish should not be kept together in community aquaria.

6. Aquaria should be kept free of sharp or abrasive objects and substances, devices in which fish may trap themselves, etc., and all such objects as shells, coral and rocks should be sterilized before introduction into aquaria.

7. Fish should be handled and disturbed as little as possible.

8. Fish should be fed regularly and not be subjected either to unvarying or capricious diets.

9. Recommended degrees of water acidity or alkalinity should be maintained.

10. Uncoated metals subject to rust, corrosion, or similar action should not be allowed to make contact with aquarium water, and the introduction of any but recommended chemicals should be rigorously avoided.

Types of Diseases. Diseases and other ailments to which tropical fish are subject include:

1. Traumatic Diseases—illnesses resulting from injuries, shock, fright, sudden changes of environment, and the like.

2. Infectious Diseases—illnesses resulting from the introduction of diseased fish or disease-carrying protozoa, bacteria, or viruses into a healthy tank.

3. Congenital Diseases—permanent hereditary malformations manifest at birth.

4. Degenerative Diseases—cancers, tumors, and various ailments brought about by the onset or prolongation of old age.

5. Parasitical Diseases—sickness, injury, or poisoning caused by the introduction of insects, fungus, or other parasites into the aquarium.

Diseases of Tropical Fish

a. *White Spot*

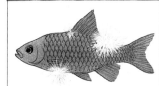

b. *Fungus*

c. *Pox*

d. *Fin and Tail Rot*

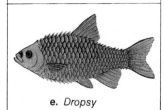

e. *Dropsy*

CAUSES AND TREATMENT OF SPECIFIC DISEASES

DISEASE	SYMPTOMS	TREATMENT
Achyla or Fungus	cottony body growths	paint affected areas with 5% methylene blue solution daily
Anchor Worms	threadlike parasites hanging from fish	immerse several hours in solution of $1/6$ grain potassium permanganate per gallon of water
Argulus	spiderlike lice hanging from fish	same as for Anchor Worms
Benedenia	fish huddle with folded fins; attempt to shake off irritants	extremely diluted solution of copper sulfate in water
Columnaris or Mouth Fungus	white line around fish's lips	250 mg chloramphenicol per gallon of water
Costiasis	lethargy, rapid breathing, poor appetite	immerse fish in 2½% salt water solution 15 min. daily
Dropsy	body swelling, protruding scales	250 mg chloramphenicol per gallon of water
Egg-binding	inability of gravid females to spawn	no effective cure known; usually fatal
Fin Congestion or Fin Rot	ragged, inflamed, or opaque fins	increase aeration; $1/60$ grain acriflavin or penicillin per gallon of water
Fluke Infection or Flatworms	paleness, gaping gills; ragged, slimy fins; panicky behavior; tendency to rub body vigorously	3 days in strong solution of methylene blue
Humpy Back	humped back	an incurable effect of senility
Ichthyophonous	multiple, often ulcerated cysts	isolate and bathe affected fish in 0.1 solution of para-chlorophenoxethol (cure unlikely)
Ichthyophthirius or "Ich" or White Spot	white spots, manifest itching	isolate fish in unplanted tank, warm water to 82-85°F., and add 5% solution of methylene blue to water

DISEASE	SYMPTOMS	TREATMENT
Itch or Saltwater Itch	manifest itching, presence of white threadlike organisms	weak solution of copper sulfate added to aquarium water
Lymphocystis	cream-colored lumpy growths	no effective medication known; isolate fish, which may recover in time
Neon Disease or Plistophora	general etiolation	no known cure
Paralytic Shock	victim stiffens and falls to bottom, or swims spasmodically after change of water	return fish to water from which it was transferred to tank
Popeye or Exophthalmos	clouded swollen eye(s)	1 drop of organic silver solution on affected area 4 times daily
Saprolegnia	cottonlike growths on open wounds	paint fish daily with 5% methylene blue solution
Sea Lice	flat ¼" parasites stick to fish (usually sea horses)	remove lice with tweezers; add methylene blue to water
Shimmy or Shimmies	victim "swims" in place	raise temperature to 85° F.; clean tank thoroughly
Shock	same as Paralytic Shock	same as for Paralytic Shock
Swim Bladder Disease	imbalance or body inversion; generally unnatural carriage	no effective treatment known
Tail Rot	ragged, inflamed, or opaque caudal fin	same as for Fin Congestion
Traumatic Diseases	visible wounds, abrasions, etc.	isolate victim in unplanted tank and treat with commercial penicillin preparation
Tuberculosis	wasting, emaciation; possible yellow spots near tail	no known cure
Velvet or Rust or Oodinium	golden powdery spots followed by circular cysts	isolate fish and treat as for Ichthophthirius
Worm Cataract	loss of eye color caused by unclean food worms	no known cure

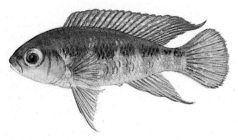

Dolphin Cichlid

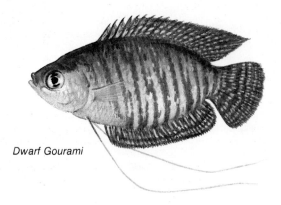

Dwarf Gourami

DOGFISH: *see* BOWFIN.

DOLPHIN CICHLID (*Aequidens itanyi*): Greenish-brown and laterally marked from its eye to the rear of its dorsal fin with an irregular dark stripe, this fair-sized fish is somewhat destructive of aquatic plants but otherwise gets along well in community aquaria. *Habitat:* Northeastern South America. *Diet:* Varied animal foods.

DORADIDAE: the taxonomic family consisting of certain heavy-bodied catfishes characteristically bearing spined bony plates on each side of the body.

DRAGONFLY LARVA: any of the young of various familiar pondside insects of the order Odonata. It frequently finds its way into home aquaria in the company of daphniae and unfortunately grows rapidly and will prey upon the smaller, more vulnerable members of a community tank. It attacks fishes from below, grasping them with retractable pincers before devouring them.

DROPSY: *see* DISEASES OF TROPICAL FISH.

DUCKWEED (*Lemna*): a floating, usually round-leaved aquatic plant favored by aquarists for its nutritive properties and for the shade it produces in top-lighted tanks.

DUSKY PIRANHA (*Pygocentrus calmoni*): a sizable, jut-jawed, sharp-toothed, rather unpleasant looking silver-gray fish. Along with other piranha species, it has gained widespread if somewhat libelous notoriety as one of the most vicious of nature's predators. Like some wolves and sharks, it can be docile enough except when aroused by the presence of fresh blood. In any event, it should be kept in isolation and handled with care. *Habitat:* Coastal regions of upper South America. *Diet:* Unwanted live fish, coarsely sliced food fish.

DWARF ARGENTINE PEARL-FISH: *see* BLACK-FINNED PEARL FISH.

DWARF AUSTRALIAN RAINBOW FISH (*Melanotaenia mac-culochi*): A popular, easily-kept fish, it tends to group with others of its kind but behaves well in community tanks. Laterally marked with seven thin stripes, the fish has yellow-edged red fins; during spawning the males develop an ephemeral but vivid yellow stripe. *Habitat:* Northern Australia. *Diet:* Varied.

DWARF CHAMELEON FISH: *see* BADIS.

DWARF GOURAMI (*Colisa lalia*): One of the most popular of the freshwater tropical fish, this small, exceedingly attractive species is easily recognizable by the males' alternating red and blue bands (paler in the females) and the relatively long dorsal and anal fins in both sexes. Peaceable and somewhat shy, it is often a target for bullying by more obstreperous species. *Habitat:* Eastern India. *Diet:* Varied.

DWARF SEA HORSE: *see* PYGMY SEA HORSE.

Dusky Piranha

E

EARTHEATER: *see* DEMON FISH.

EARTHWORM: any of various annelid worms, usually of the family Lubricidae, used as food for both freshwater and marine tropical fish.

EEL: (1) Any of numerous serpentlike marine or freshwater fishes of the order Anguilliformes (Apodes). (2) Any of several tropical fishes, including the so-called spiny eels of the family Mastacembelidae, which despite their eellike shapes are not in fact true eels but are popularly so termed.

EEL CATFISH (*Channallabes apus*): This good-sized, snakelike, dark-brown catfish is mostly nocturnal and perpetually hungry. Best kept in community tanks only while still young. *Habitat:* Central Africa. *Diet:* Varied, with meaty foods much preferred.

EGG-BINDING: *see* DISEASES OF TROPICAL FISH.

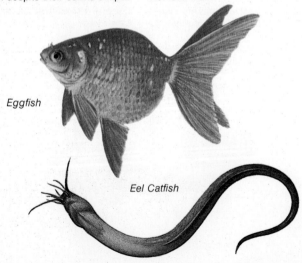

Eggfish

Eel Catfish

EGG-BURIERS: those members of the family Cyprinodontidae commonly called "annual" fishes (e.g., the BLACK-FINNED PEARL-FISH), which bury their eggs in mud before dying of asphyxia when the water in which they swim evaporates during the dry season. In captivity, they will bury their eggs in peat moss.

EGGFISH: a variety of *Carassius auratus* (*see* GOLDFISH) distinguishable by its ruddy coloration, ovoid body, and lack of dorsal fin.

EGG-HANGERS: those members of the family Cyprinodontidae, including the various "panchax" species, which in their natural habitats lay their eggs on the roots of floating plants. In captivity, spawning is encouraged by use of a breeding mop, a floating device made up of rootlike strands of nylon or similar materials.

EGG-LAYING TOOTH CARPS: the popular designation for the various members of the family Cyprinodontidae.

EGYPTIAN MOUTHBREEDER (or **MOUTHBROODER**) (*Haplochromis multicolor*): The unusual feature of this small, inaccurately-named cichlid is that as soon as its eggs are laid they are gathered up by the female, who keeps them in her mouth until they have not only hatched, but the fry have absorbed the yolk sac. As its Latin name suggests, the fish's coloration is variable. Ill behaved in community aquaria. *Habitat:* Nigeria. *Diet:* Varied, with meaty foods and some herbaceous matter preferred, and with considerable loss of appetite during the brooding period.

EINTHOVEN'S RASBORA: *see* BRILLIANT RASBORA.

ELECTRIC CATFISH (*Malapterurus electricus*): Not often kept by hobbyists but popular in public aquaria, this large gray African catfish can discharge a moderately powerful electric current, the purpose of which is a matter of some dispute. A ruthless predator, it should be kept in isolation from other species. *Habitat:* Tropical Africa. *Diet:* Live fish.

ELEPHANT-NOSE or **ELEPHANT FISH:** any of various members of the family Mormyridae, native to Africa and distinguishable by a drooping, trunk-like snout.

ELONGATED HATCHETFISH (*Triportheus elongatus*): a peaceable, fairly good-sized, indistinctly marked silvery fish whose distinguishing feature is the attenuation of the central dark-colored rays of the caudal fin. *Habitat:* Upper South America. *Diet:* Small live foods preferred.

Electric Catfish

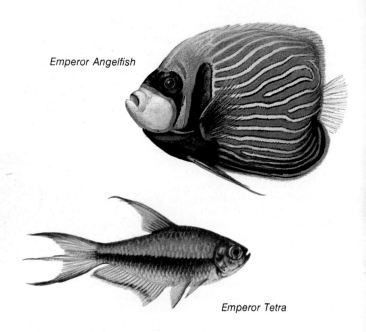

Emperor Angelfish

Emperor Tetra

EMPEROR ANGELFISH (*Pomacanthus imperator*): a good-sized marine fish marked with alternating blue-purple and pale yellow stripes (vertical from the snout to the middle of the body, and then concentric to the base of the caudal fin) on a black ground. Hardy but aggressive. *Habitat:* Western Pacific Ocean. *Diet:* Small live foods, chopped shrimp, brine shrimp. NOTE: Some confusion in nomenclature exists concerning this fish and several other marine angelfishes. One authority, for example, not only illustrates an altogether dissimilar species under the same name, but gives koran (the usual common designation for *Pomacanthus semicir-*

culatus) as one of its popular names.

EMPEROR TETRA (*Nematobrycon palmeri*): The female of this species, although small herself, is considerably larger than the male. Marked with a dark horizontal stripe that runs most of its body length, it is a shy but hardy fish. It is easily bred, and the courtship ritual entails much tremulous movement of the male's fins. *Habitat:* Colombia. *Diet:* Varied, with small live foods preferred.

EVOLUTION OF FISHES: Water is responsible for more erasures than any other physical substance. Unfortunately for the ichthyologist, the natural habitat—the only habitat—of the fish is water and, consequently, the record of piscatorial life on this planet has been largely washed away. From the relatively few fossil remains that have survived the reductive work of time, a certain evolutionary chain of events can be traced in its rough outlines. And from these out- lines we can see that the various warm-blooded birds and mammals evolved from cold-blooded reptilian forms, in turn descended from amphibians whose immediate ancestors were fish and *whose* progenitors were rudimentary vertebrates derived from invertebrate forerunners. Further

Xiphactinus Audax fish was over 12 feet long.

Holoptychius

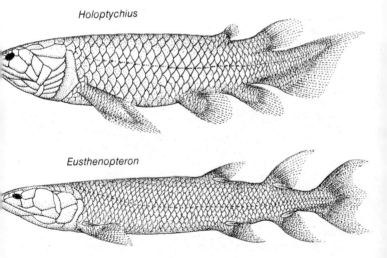

Eusthenopteron

Piscara pealie fossil fish found in Green River Shale in Wyoming.

fossil evidence, scanty as it may be, suggests that the 20,000 or more species of fishes known to exist today are by far the lesser part of the near-infinitude of fishes that have existed since the dawn of life on earth. Soft-bodied organisms play an evanescent role in prehistory and whatever links may have existed between the earliest larval vertebrates and the protofishes have long since been erased by tides stilled aeons ago. The oldest fishes that we know are little different from those that swim today. At that point when man picks up the thread, though, the great armored fishes were already extinct and the others—the jawless, cartilaginous, and bony

Fossil fish in shale believed to be 40 to 50 million years old.

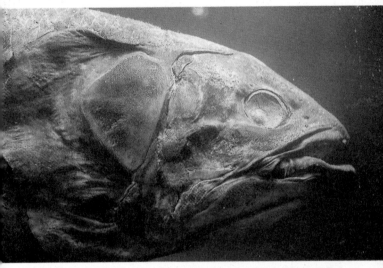

This coelacanth is one of a very ancient group of fishes which first appeared 300 million years ago. One of this amazing species was caught alive in 1938 off the tip of Africa.

fishes—were much as we now find them: the first two classes headed inevitably for extinction; the third, changeable, adaptable, viable, flourishing in countless environments it was never made to live in.

EXCLAMATION-POINT RAS-BORA or **OCELLATED DWARF RASBORA** (*Rasbora uroph-thalma*): Named for the tapering

blue lateral stripe that runs from behind the eye to culminate in a round spot at the base of the caudal fin, this small, peaceable rasbora is best kept in a tank where larger species will not bother it. Active and easy to breed. *Habitat:* Sumatra. *Diet:* Varied small foods.

EXOPTHALMIA or **POP-EYE:** *see* DISEASES OF TROPICAL FISH.

Exclamation-Point Rasbora

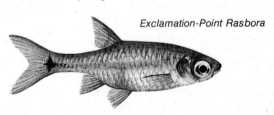

F

FANTAIL GOLDFISH: a variety of *Carassius auratus* (*see* GOLDFISH) distinguished by the elaborate development of its gracefully elongated caudal fins.

FEATHERTAIL TETRA: *see* CONGO TETRA.

FEEDING OF TROPICAL FISH: Like all animals, fish subsist on a diet of proteins, fats, carbohydrates, vitamins, and minerals. Given stable conditions, the tropical fish in its natural habitat will provide itself with a balanced, healthful diet comprised roughly of the requisite amounts of these nutrients. In most cases, it is hardly possible for the home aquarist to duplicate with any degree of exactitude the natural diets of the various species. Every attempt should be made, nonetheless, to provide tropical fishes with diets as closely analagous as possible to those they enjoy in nature. On its face, this may seem a difficult task, since all too little is known of the natural feeding habits of most tropical fish, whose divers diets may be made up of flora and fauna unavailable outside their native haunts. Fortunately, however, tropical fish, like most creatures except man, tend to feed sensibly if permitted to, in-

stinctively shunning what is bad for them and showing marked preferences for those foods that are most nutritious. Moreover, most species are quite adaptable and willingly will accept foods that have no close counterparts in their natural environments, so long as those foods answer their needs. Such substances as beef heart, spinach, oatmeal, and the yolks of hard-boiled eggs, for example, are in rather short supply in the world's seas, streams, and ponds; all, however, play useful dietary roles in the home aquarium.

In each of its articles on particular species of tropical fish, this book recommends the foods most suitable to the species under discussion. For any species not specifically covered, the logical course is for the aquarist to offer the fish a diet made up of foods recommended for a related species. A certain amount of trial and error (error on the aquarist's part, not the fish's) may be involved here, but the important thing is for the fish, not the human, to be allowed to make the ultimate dietary decisions. Given no options, a strict carnivore may accept a diet made up exclusively of cereals, but it will soon be a most unhappy and un-

Micro-worms

Blood Worms

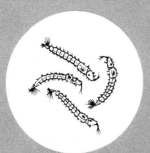

Glass Worms

Tubifex Worms

Grindal Worms

White Worms

healthy fish. Similarly, a largely herbivorous fish is being done a distinct disservice by the well-meaning aquarist who serves it nothing but shrimp that may be too costly for his own table.

In general, fish prefer their proteins in the form of live food—*Tubifex, Daphnia*, mosquito larvae, smaller fish, brine shrimp, whiteworms, and the like. Several of these foodstuffs can be collected or cultivated by the home aquarist and, after a nominal initial cash outlay, provide a cheap, convenient source of healthful nutrients. A summary of the more widely used standard aquarium foods follows.

FOODS FOR FRY: However voracious it may appear to be, the newborn child is not usually served a sirloin steak and a baked potato for its first meal. Unfortunately, though, many aquarists, misled by the apparent precociousness of newly hatched fry, will serve them comparable fare from the start. But while they may resemble their parents in every respect but size, the fry of most tropical fish have small mouths and delicate digestive tracts and should be fed accordingly. Recommended food for fry:

Infusoria (singular: infusorian): Any of numerous microscopic organisms, particularly of the phylum Protozoa or the order Rotifera. Infusoria can be collected from stagnant ponds, where they appear as a green cloud, or cultivated. Cultivation is achieved by placing a bit of bruised lettuce or spinach or some chapped hay in a jar of tap water to which some aged aquarium water has been added. The solution is then kept at 76° F. for 48 hours or more, after which time it is ready for use.

Egg Yolk: The yellow of a hard-boiled egg, crumbled and introduced into the aquarium, produces a cloud of miniscule particles suitable for newly hatched fry.

Dry Foods: Various dried foods, ground to a fine powder, are suitable for small fry. Innumerable commercial preparations are available, but aquarists lacking easy access to aquarium supply houses may prepare their own dry foods by finely powdering such substances as cereals, dog biscuits, dried shrimp, cod flakes, dried parsley, and the like.

Brine Shrimp (*Artemia salina*): An aquarium staple, brine shrimp are particularly suitable for large-mouthed fry and most adult fish. Commercially available in live, dried, and frozen form, they may be cultivated by immersing brine shrimp eggs (available at most aquarium supply shops) in slightly saline water warmed for 48 hours at 80° F.

Micro-worms (*Anguilluda silusia*): Diminutive nematode worms, they are easily raised by obtaining an initial culture (from a fellow aquarist or an aquarium supply shop) and introducing it into a 1-inch layer of 4 parts cooked oatmeal or pablum to 1 part yeast, diluting the mixture with water and maintaining at 70 to 80° F.

Grindal worms (*Enchytraeus buchholzi*): Suitable for larger fry and smaller adults, these diminutive worms may be raised at temperatures above 70° F. from commercially available cultures.

STANDARD AQUARIUM FOODS: All the above are suitable for most growing and mature fish. Some large marine angelfishes, however, should not be fed baby brine shrimp which, for them, constitute a gill irritant. Other standard foods:

Daphnia: Any of numerous minute freshwater crustaceans of the genus *Daphnia*, these, along with slightly smaller crustacean *Cyclops*, are commonly termed "water fleas" and are considered by many aquarists to be the ideal fish food. *Daphnia* should not be used indiscriminately, however, for several reasons: they have a distinct laxative effect, and should be balanced with starchy binding foods to prevent weight loss and general weakening in fish; they lead some species of tropical fish to overestimate their capacities and gorge themselves dangerously; they are often accompanied by dangerous parasites; their native waters are often infested with disease-bearing microorganisms. *Daphnia* are available commercially in live, dried, and frozen form, and may be collected in fine mesh nets from ponds rich in decaying matter, where they usually appear as a greenish, grayish, or red-orange cloud on warm, humid days.

Gnat and Mosquito Larvae: Usually found in close proximity to *Daphnia* during the summer months, these organisms are nutritious but should not be overfed to fish lest uneaten larvae hatch and escape the aquarium. Particularly favored by tooth-carps and live-bearers, they are sold in most aquarium supply shops.

Tubifex: Slender, threadlike red worms, *Tubifex* are a nourishing food, but must be thoroughly washed in running water for 48 hours before being fed to fish. Commercially available live or frozen, they can be found in streams rich in organic matter, where they partially burrow, head-downward, into mud bottoms.

Whiteworms (*Enchytraeus albidus*): Easily raised by the aquarist in commercially prepared or homemade culture media, these inch-long creatures are nutritious, but their extremely high fat content can cause obesity if fish. In home cultivation, worm cultures (available at aquarium supply houses) are intoduced into moist aggregates of soil, peat, and sand, or similar substances, covered, kept in a dark place at 55° F., and fed commercially prepared foods or baby cereals.

Freshwater Shrimp: Various small crustaceans found under stones or among vegetation in running streams, these are a nutritious food for larger fish.

Live Unwanted Fish: Many aquarists cultivate common guppies or other small, inexpensive tropical fish as food for larger carnivorous species. Domestic minnows and similar creatures serve the same purpose, but should be quarantined for a time before use.

Beef Heart and Liver: Excellent for many species, these foods should be hacked, chopped, or minced, depending on the size and capacity of the fish. Liver should be poached in water until the blood coagulates, so that it does not cloud the aquarium.

Chopped fresh Shrimp: One of

the most satisfactory of all aquarium foods, it can be served cooked or raw and is very popular with many species, particularly marine fishes.

Other good aquarium foods include green algae, leaf lettuce, spinach, and similar greens, whole or chopped earthworms, glass or phantom larvae, washed minced clams, drayfish, bloodworms, fish roe, and, for various marine species, crushed sea urchins, unshelled chopped shrimp small crabs, snails, live coral, mussels, live plankton, live insects, and occasional pinches of paprika for color tone.

FILTRATION AND FILTERS: *see* AQUARIUM CARE AND MANAGEMENT.

FIN CONGESTION: *see* DISEASES OF TROPICAL FISH.

FINGERFISH: *see* MALAYAN ANGEL.

FIN ROT: *see* DISEASES OF TROPICAL FISH.

FIRE-MOUTH or **FIRE-MOUTH CICHLID** (*Cichlasoma meeki*): One of the most popular of the cichlids and one of the best-behaved, this handsome, moderate-sized fish takes its popular name from the distinctive red flush that begins around the mouth and often extends backward and downward over much of the lower portion of its blue-gray body. Usually quite peaceable, it will spawn in community tanks, but can be unpredictable during the mating period, at which time it has been known to inflict serious injury even on much larger tankmates. *Habitat:* Upper Yucatan Peninsula, Mexico. *Diet:* Small live foods.

FIRE-MOUTH PANCHAX or **REDJAW KILLIE** (*Epiplatys chaperi* or *Panchax chaperi*): One of the hardy EGG-HANGERS, which spawn readily and prolifically, this flat-headed little killie takes its popular names from the red marking on the underside of the male's

Fire-Mouth

Flame Tetra

Fire-Mouth Panchax

jaw. *Habitat:* West Africa. *Diet:* Small live foods.

FLAG CICHLID or **THAYER'S CICHLID** (*Aequidens curviceps*): Rather small and quite peaceable for a cichlid, this is an attractive brownish-green fish with traces of blue between the dorsal and anal fins and with brighter blue spots on the caudal fin. Suitable for community aquaria. *Habitat:* Amazon River region. *Diet:* Small live foods, finely chopped earthworms.

FLAME TETRA or **RED TETRA** (*Hyphessobrycon flammeus*): Sometimes called "Tet from Rio," this very small characin is one of the most beautiful species known to aquarists. Shading from a coppery red, around the head and gill vicinity, to a rich ruby, it bears a pair of dark vertical marks behind the gill cover. Peaceable and gregarious, it should be kept with other small species and, preferably, in small schools. *Habitat:* Vicinity of Rio de Janeiro, Brazil. *Diet:* Small live or frozen foods.

FLATWORMS or **FLUKES:** *see* DISEASES OF TROPICAL FISH.

FLYING BARB (*Esomus danrica* or *E. danricus*): Very active, much drawn to the surface, and equipped with exceptionally wide pectoral fins, this is an accomplished jumper and must be kept in a covered tank. Silver-gray and marked with a dark horizontal line, the fish usually glows with a violet sheen and is readily distinguishable by the elongated barbels that flow from the upper lip to the middle of the body. Best displayed in schools under good illumination. *Habitat:* Northeastern India, Burma. *Diet:* Small live foods that

Four-Eyed Butterfly Fish

Flying Fox

tend to swim on or just beneath the surface of the water.

FLYING FOX (*Epalzeorhynchus kallopterus*): One of the handsomest of the useful scavengers, this sizable and peaceable creature is a welcome addition to community tanks, where it goes about its own business, rooting in the bottom for edible matter. Striped laterally and boldly in gold on a brown-green ground, it has not been bred in captivity and consequently is rather hard to come by. *Habitat:* Sumatra, Borneo. *Diet:* Varied, with herbaceous matter —green algae in particular— preferred.

FOUR-BARRED TIGER FISH (*Datnioides quadrifasciatus*): Although quite large, this handsome fish is not aggressive, but may mistake smaller tankmates for food. It is not four-barred, as its name implies, but bears as many as ten vertical bands which tend to coalesce as the fish ages. *Habitat:* India, Burma, Thailand, Australia. *Diet:* Unwanted small fish, larger live foods, coarsely chopped shrimp.

FOUR-EYED BUTTERFLY FISH (*Chaetodon capistratus*): This hardy, popular, subtly marked marine fish bears a very convincing ocellus, or false eye, at the caudal base—a camouflage device meant to deceive predators apparently on the theory that it is preferable to be devoured going than coming. A sort of herringbone pattern covers most of the disclike body and a bold vertical stripe angles through the eye. *Habitat:* Florida coastal waters. *Diet:* Live tubifex worms much preferred, with similar foods taken reluctantly. NOTE: Often a difficult feeder until habituated to its diet.

FRENCH ANGELFISH (*Pomacanthus paru*): Much like the black angelfish (*P. arcuatus*), this striking marine fish is prized by collectors for the beauty of its gold-flecked scales and because its brilliant yellow bands do not fade with age as rapidly as do those of *P. arcuatus*. Another distinctive characteristic is its habit of swimming in a somewhat vacillating circular pattern. *Habitat:* Atlantic coastal waters from Florida to Brazil. *Diet:* Brine shrimp in a more or less steady supply for smaller specimens, chopped or whole earthworms and meaty foods for larger fish; paprika for color.

FRESHWATER SHRIMP (*Gammarus pulex*): a crustacean commonly found in running streams and used as food for the larger tropical fishes.

FRY: any small fish, usually a recently hatched one.

FUNGUS: *see* DISEASES OF TROPICAL FISH.

GAMBUSINOS or **LIVE-BEARING TOOTH CARPS:** *see* POECILIIDAE.

GARNET TETRA (*Hemigrammus pulcher*): a small, peaceable, well-behaved characin whose greenish body is burnished with golden metallic glints. It bears a large black and smaller red mark on the rear third of its body, both ending at the base of the caudal fin. It needs warmth, does not breed readily, and is best displayed in groups or schools. *Habitat:* Upper Amazon River. *Diet:* Varied, with small live foods preferred.

GASPING: *see* DISEASES OF TROPICAL FISH.

GASTEROSTEIDAE: *see* STICKLEBACK.

GERY'S APHYOSEMION (*Aphyosemion gery*): one of the most beautiful of all the KILLIFISH, the male has a deep blue body marked with a series of bright-red slanting bars irregularly interspersed with spots of the same color; its graceful caudal fin is edged with bright yellow. Does very well in confined spaces. *Habitat:* West Africa. *Diet:* Small live foods, with frozen foods taken reluctantly.

GIANT DANIO (*Danio malabaricus*): Although fairly large, this very popular species is peaceable and well behaved in community aquaria, and its hardiness and

Gery's Aphyosemion

readiness to breed further enhances its attractiveness. Its light-blue body is marked with lateral gray-blue stripes separated by narrower yellow lines. *Habitat:* Western India, Sri Lanka. *Diet:* Varied.

GIANT GOURAMI or **STRIPED GOURAMI** (*Colisa fasciata*): a handsome, colorfully banded, rather shy species, it is easily bred and adapts well to life in community aquaria. Blue highlights shimmer over its red-brown body, which is similar in its markings to that of the dwarf gourami (*Colisa lalia*). *Habitat:* India, Burma. *Diet:* Varied, with small live foods preferred.

GLASS BLOODFIN: *see* TRANSLUCENT BLOODFIN.

GLASS CATFISH (*Kryptoterus bicirrhis*): Resembling a living X-ray picture, this highly transparent species is not a scavenger, as

are most catfishes, and thrives on the company of its own kind. *Habitat:* India, the Greater Sunda Islands. *Diet:* Small live foods.

GLASSFISH (*Chanda lala*): This small, hardy chandid is much prized for its prismatic translucence. Not easily bred, it thrives best in slightly brackish water. *Habitat:* India. *Diet:* Small live foods exclusively.

GLASS LARVAE or **PHANTOM LARVAE**: the transparent larvae of the fly *Corethra plumicornis*, frequently used in aquaria as food. NOTE: Dangerous to young fry.

GLOWLIGHT TETRA (*Hemigrammus erythrozonus* or *H. gracilis*): one of the commonest and most beautiful of aquarium fishes, it has a translucent olive-green body transversely divided by a refulgent red or purple stripe that seems almost incandescent in certain lights. Best displayed under

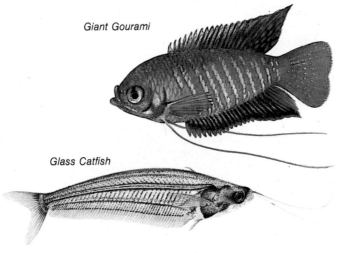

Giant Gourami

Glass Catfish

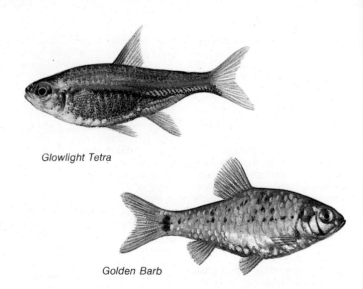

Glowlight Tetra

Golden Barb

subdued illumination and in small schools, it gets along well with other small characins. *Habitat:* British Guiana and its environs. *Diet:* Ordinary aquarium foods.

GOATFISH: any of some 50 species comprising the family MULLIDAE.

GOBIIDAE: loosely, the largest of several taxonomically related families of some 600 freshwater, marine or brackish-water gobies, including the sleeper gobies (Family Eleotridae) and the loach gobies (Family Microdesmidae), characteristically small in size and equipped with fused pelvic fins and two dorsal fins.

GOBY: any fish of the families Eleotridae, Gobiidae, or Periophthalmidae, including such species as the mud skipper (*Periopthalmus barbarus*) and bumblebeefish (*Brachygobius*

xanthozona), collectively known as the gobies.

GOLDEN BARB (*Puntius saschi*): a very popular aquarium fish, medium sized, easily bred, well mannered, and quite active. Its metallic golden body bears a dark horizontal bar (indistinct on the female) and red or red-orange fins. *Habitat:* Malay Peninsula. *Diet:* Ordinary aquarium foods.

GOLDEN DOUBLE SWORD GUPPY: a hybrid elaboration of the common GUPPY (*Lebistes reticulatus*), prized for its golden color and the attenuated points on its caudal fin.

GOLDEN-EYED DWARF CICHLID (*Nannacara anomala*): The female of this species is half the size of the male, which itself usually does not exceed 3 inches in length. Although neither sex is particularly striking (the male's sweeping dorsal and anal fins and metallic yellow-green sheen make it somewhat more noticeable than its nondescript mate), the species is quite popular because of its readiness to spawn in very small aquaria. *Habitat:* British Guiana. *Diet:* Small live and ground meaty foods.

GOLDEN PHEASANT or **GOLDEN PHEASANT GULARIS** (*Roloffia occidentalis*): Formerly known as *Aphyosemion sjoestedti,* this is an egg-burier whose spawn has been known to incubate in its natural habitat for as long as 6 months during prolonged dry seasons. It is a beautifully marked, multicolored KILLIFISH, but does not adapt well to community aquaria. *Habitat:* West African coast from Dakar almost to the Equator. *Diet:* Varied live foods.

GOLDEN WAGTAIL: a popular variety of the PLATY (*Xiphophorous maculatus*) esteemed for its bright golden color.

GOLDFISH (*Carassius auratus*): The best-known and most extensively cultivated member of the family Cyprinidae and, indeed, of aquarium fishes in general, this perennially popular carp was domesticated in China a millennium or more ago. Since that time

Eggfish – a common variety of Gold fish

innumerable fancy and often quite grotesque varieties have been developed through selective breeding. Not a true tropical fish, the goldfish originated in China and now can be found throughout the temperate zones. A hardy, extremely adaptable fish, it can be kept indoors or out, will fend for itself in outdoor pools, and has been known to withstand climatic conditions ranging from iced-over ponds to importation into the tropics. Most favorably displayed in isolation from other species (where they are also safe from fin-nippers). The broader varietal categories of goldfish include the fantail, lionhead, comet, and celes-

Golden Pheasant

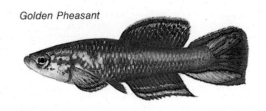

Celestial Goldfish

Many fishes belonging to the goldfish family are otherwise named.

Eggfish

Koi

Comet Goldfish.

Lionhead Goldfish

Shubunkim

95

tial goldfishes, the eggfish, shubunkin, and many others, most of which can be divided into narrower, more refined categories. *Habitat:* Originally China, now widespread throughout the world. *Diet:* Extremely varied.

GONOPODIUM: *see* ANATOMY.

GOURAMI (*Osphronemus goramy*): a very large, thick-lipped anabantid used primarily as a food fish in its native regions. It has a dark-speckled yellowish body and is somewhat better suited to public aquaria and fish markets than to hobbyists' tanks. *Habitat:* Greater Sunda Islands and vicinity. *Diet:* Chopped crustaceans and mollusks, herbaceous matter, cereals.

GREAT DIVING BEETLE (*Dytiscus marginalis*): an insect predator often introduced into home aquaria in larval form along with the daphniae whose ponds it frequents. Equipped with large, powerful jaws through which it injects digestive juices that "tenderize" its prey, it is capable, even in larval form, of killing small aquarium fishes.

GREEN DISCUS (*Symphysodon aequifasciata a.*): Perhaps the most beautiful and stately of the cichlids, this large, pancake-shaped, olive-green creature is marked with nine often indistinct vertical bars and wavy blue horizontal streaks resembling schematic representations of flowing water. Difficult to breed, they make peaceable adornments to community aquaria, but require soft, acid water. *Habitat:* Brazil. *Diet:* Varied live foods, frozen beef heart.

GREEN LACE GUPPY: An elaborated variety of the common GUPPY (*Lebistes reticulatus*), it is prized for the lacelike patterns on its body and tail.

GREEN SWORDTAIL: A variety of the SWORDTAIL or helleri (*Xiphophorus helleri*), it is colored a more-or-less uniform olive-green.

GRINDAL WORM (*Enchytraeus buchholtzi*): Similar to the whiteworm, its small size makes it a staple food for growing fry of species that thrive on small live foods.

Green Discus

Green Swordtail

Guppy

GROUPER: The popular name for any of numerous marine fishes of the family SERRANIDAE.

GUPPY (*Lebistes reticulatus*): The best-known and by far the most popular of the ovoviviparous or live-bearing, fishes, the guppy probably has introduced more aquarists to their hobby than all the other tropical fishes combined. Physically attractive, active, prodigiously fertile, extremely hardy, altogether peaceable, and capable of thriving in almost any temperature, confined spaces, and near-stagnant water, it is the ideal "beginner's" species. In its almost infinite variety, it retains interest even for the most sophisticated collectors. Hybridized in countless combinations and permutations, most of the guppies commercially available today bear little or no resemblance to the nondescript wild guppy from which they derive. Selective breeding has resulted in such strains as the lyretail, sword-tail, and veiltail guppies, which are much admired for their spectacular fin development and the splendor of their coloration. *Habitat:* West Indies, Venezuela, the Guianas, northern Brazil. *Diet:* Varied, with frequent small feedings recommended.

GYMNOTIDAE: *see* KNIFE FISH.

Guppy—fin shapes:

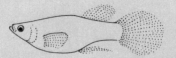

a. *Robson-Roundtail*

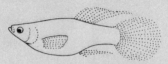

b. *Roundtail*

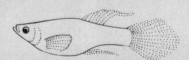

c. *Spade or Cofertail*

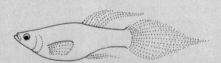

d. *Pointed or Speartail*

e. *Top Sword*

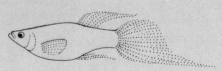

f. *Bottom Sword*

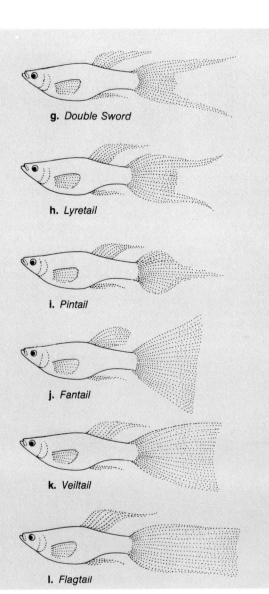

g. *Double Sword*

h. *Lyretail*

i. *Pintail*

j. *Fantail*

k. *Veiltail*

l. *Flagtail*

H

HALF-BANDED BARB (*Capoeta semifasciolatus*): a greenish-brown medium-sized species in which the females are somewhat larger·than the males. The fish's vertical bars extend only about halfway down its body. *Habitat:* Southern China. *Diet:* Varied.

HALF-BANDED LOACH (*Acanthophthalmus semicinctus*): Very similar to and often confused with the coolie loach, this shy seminocturnal scavenger is well suited to community tanks, but is easily bruised by coarse gravel, sharp stones, or other rough materials. *Habitat:* Greater and Lesser Sunda Islands. *Diet:* Small live foods, tank detritus.

HALF-BANDED PIKE CICHLID (*Crenicichla geayi*): A good-sized, voracious, and extremely efficient predator, this olive-green creature is equipped with a traplike under-slung jaw and a dorsal fin that traverses most of its elongated body. It is marked from snout to caudal fin by a dark horizontal stripe, above which it bears a series of vertical bars. Altogether unsuitable in community tanks. *Habitat:* Central Amazon River and vicinity. *Diet:* Live fish, earthworms.

HALF-BEAK (*Dermgenys pusillus*): Fond of brackish water and distinguishable by its protuberant, beaklike lower jaw, this small gray

Half-Banded Loach

Half-Banded Pike Cichlid

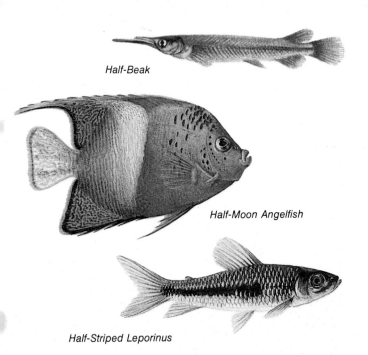

Half-Beak

Half-Moon Angelfish

Half-Striped Leporinus

surface swimmer is one of the few live-bearers found outside the New World. *Habitat:* Thailand, the Malay Archipelego. *Diet:* Small live foods, with daphniae, mosquito larvae, and young brine shrimp preferred.

HALF-LINED HEMIODUS (*Hemiodus semitaeniatus*): A long, slender, well-muscled, accomplished jumper, it is peaceable and makes a lively, attractive addition to community tanks. Rather colorless, it bears horizontal exclamation-pointlike markings that begin below and slightly behind the short dorsal fin and extend through the lower lobe of the caudal fine.

Habitat: The Guianas and Amazon Basin. *Diet:* Dry foods, herbaceous matter.

HALF-MOON ANGELFISH (*Pomacanthus maculosus*). Although inclined to become somewhat etiolated as' it matures, this large, unusual marine fish is quite striking when young, with a brilliant marking, shaped like a crescent moon, in the center of its blue-purple body. *Habitat:* Red Sea, western Indian Ocean. *Diet:* Varied.

HALF-STRIPED LEPORINUS (*Leporinus agassizi*): a large, peaceful, clearly marked but not very colorful fish, it bears a horizontal stripe on the rear half of its

Harlequin Fish

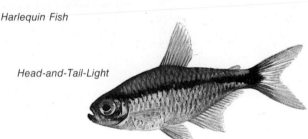

Head-and-Tail-Light

body and spends much of its time grazing on algae. *Habitat:* Central Amazon region. *Diet:* Varied, with a marked preference for herbaceous matter.

HANCOCK'S AMBLYDORAS (*Amblydoras hancockii*): This sizable mottled brown, white-striped spiny catfish is a nocturnal species and should be provided with dark hiding places. *Habitat:* The Guianas and western Amazon region. *Diet:* Small live foods.

HARD-LIPPED BARB (*Osteochilus hasselti*): A common food fish in its native haunts, this peaceable creature thrives best in a tank of dimensions commensurate with its considerable size. Marked with horizontally aligned spots, it is silver-gray with occasional yellow glints. *Habitat:* Southeast Asia, the Malay Archipelego. *Diet:* Live foods, herbaceous matter.

HARLEQUIN FISH (*Rasbora heteromorpha*): One of the most popular of all aquarium fishes, this small, striking creature is much blunter in shape than most rasboras and bears a large, intensely black triangle, the outline of which follows the contours of the rear half of its otherwise red body. Peaceable, active, and very decorative in a community tank, it "hangs" its eggs from the undersides of leaves. *Habitat:* Malay Peninsula, Sumatra, Java. *Diet:* Varied, with small live foods preferred.

HART'S RIVULUS (*Rivulus harti*): Frequently confused with the smaller golden rivulus (*R. urophthalmus*), this relatively peaceable jumper ranges in color from gray to pink to blue-green. The fish is marked with horizontal rows of dots, bright red in the male and dull red or red-brown in the female. *Habitat:* Northwestern South

America, Trinidad. *Diet:* Live foods. NOTE: Should be kept with fishes its own size or larger.

HAWKFISH: the popular designation for the various marine species belonging to the family CIRRHITIDAE, of which such members as the freckled hawkfish (*Paracirrhites forsteri*) and spotted hawkfish (*Cirrhitichthys aprinus*) are popular collectors' items.

HEAD-AND-TAIL-LIGHT (*Hemigrammus ocellifer*): Formerly known as "beacon fish," this small, extremely popular tetra has luminous golden-red eyes and a glowing tail-spot to make up for its relatively colorless body. Shown to best advantage in small schools and under top lighting, it is a pleasant, attractive, adaptable, easily bred creature that gets along well with fishes its own size and prefers rather warm water. *Habitat:* British Guiana and the Amazon River region. *Diet:* Varied, with small live foods preferred.

HEATERS: *see* AQUARIUM CARE AND MANAGEMENT.

HELLERI: *see* SWORDTAIL.

HEMIGRAMMUS: a genus of characins native to the Amazon basin, of which the best known are the glowlight tetra, head-and-tail-light and silver-tip tetra. Named for the incomplete lateral line characteristic of its various species.

HEMIRHAMPHIDAE: the taxonomic family comprising the HALF-BEAK and related species.

HERMIT CRAB: any of various crustaceans of the order Decapoda, lacking armor on the abdomen and occupying the vacant shells of univalve mollusks. Several species of hermit crabs are popular with marine aquarists, who value them for their scavenging propensities.

HIGH HAT: *see* CUBBYU.

HOGFISH: (1) *Bodianus pulchellus*, a deep-water marine food fish commonly called scarlet hogfish or Cuban hogfish, colored a brilliant red and yellow and popular with those saltwater aquarists who collect larger species. (2) *Bodianus rufus*, or Spanish hogfish, a large, slender blue-and-yellow fish from shallow waters.

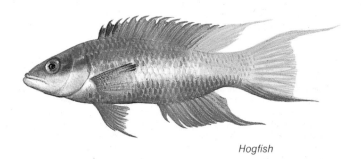

Hogfish

Hora's Loach

Habitat (both): Florida coastal and Caribbean waters. *Diet* (both): Minced shrimp, small live foods, fish roe.

HOLOCENTRIDAE: the taxonomic family comprising the various marine squirrel fishes, characterized by their predominately red coloration and spiny body coverings.

HONEY GOURAMI or **HONEY DWARF GOURAMI** or **SUNSET GOURAMI** (*Colisa chunae*): The color of dark honey except for its dark-blue head and underside and yellow-edged dorsal fin, this small, peaceable bubble-nest builder breeds readily when the quite high water temperatures it normally prefers are lowered to around 75°F. *Habitat:* Eastern India. *Diet:* Small live foods, with young brine shrimp preferred.

HOPLO: *see* CASCUDO.

HORA'S LOACH (*Botia horae*): This shy, medium-sized nocturnal loach is of a yellow-green color and bears a striking black stripe that begins at the snout and transverses the entire back before plunging downward across the base of the caudal fin. *Habitat:* Thailand. *Diet:* Varied, with small live foods and tank detritus preferred.

HORSESHOE CRAB: any of several marine arthropods of the class Merostomata, having a large, round domed body and a long lancelike tail. The young of smaller species sometimes are introduced into marine aquaria, where they thrive best when bits of finely minced fish or crustaceans are pushed under their shells as they rest on the bottom.

HUMMINGBIRD FISH or **MYERS' LAMPEYE** (*Aplocheilichthys myersi*): a tiny, brilliantly iridescent, quick-moving creature shown to best advantage in large schools and not very successfully kept in community aquaria. Olive-green with a vivid blue sheen, the male has a longer, more colorful dorsal fin than the female. *Habitat:* Congo. *Diet:* Small live foods.

HUMPBACK LIMIA or **HUNCHBACK LIMIA** (*Limia nigrofasciata*): an attractive gambusino species in which the male's shape alters considerably with maturity, with the back developing a pronounced hump and the dorsal fin enlarging to a marked degree. Small, colored grayish-to-olive,

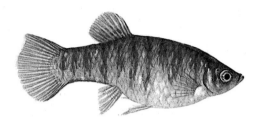
Humpback Limia

bearing about ten vertical bands on its sides, and translucent enough to reveal shadowy traces of its skeletal structure, it is peaceful toward other species but often cannibalizes its young. Prefers very warm water. *Habitat:* Haiti, Dominican Republic. *Diet:* Varied, with prepared foods preferred.

HUMPY BACK: *see* DISEASES OF TROPICAL FISH.

HYBRIDS and **HYBRIDIZATION:** *see* BREEDING TROPICAL FISHES.

HYDRA: any of various small freshwater polyps having tubelike bodies and mouths surrounded by whiplike tentacles. Often unwittingly introduced into aquaria, where they can do damage to smaller fish, they are in turn preyed upon by gouramis and guppies.

HYDROMETER: *see* WATER.

ICHTHYOLOGY: that branch of zoology concerned with fishes.

ICHTHYOPHONUS: *see* DISEASES OF TROPICAL FISH.

ICHTHYOPHTHIRIUS or **"ICH":** *see* DISEASES OF TROPICAL FISH.

INDIAN HATCHETFISH (*Laubuca laubuca*): Despite its name, this is not related to the various characin hatchetfishes of South America, but is a member of the family Cyprinidae. Medium-sized, with an iridescent blue-green body, it is a lively swimmer and accomplished jumper and should not be left in an uncovered tank.

Habitat: India, Burma, Malay Peninsula, Sumatra. *Diet:* Varied, with floating foods preferred.

INFUSORIA (*singular:* infusorian): any of numerous microscopic organisms found in stagnant water and used as food for tropical fish and their fry. Among the more familiar infusoria are the paramecium, euglena, and chlamydomonas. Home aquarists can prepare infusoria by incubating bits of crushed lettuce leaf in a mixture of fresh water and aged tank water for 48 hours at 76°F.

ITCH or **SALT WATER ITCH:** *see* DISEASES OF TROPICAL FISH.

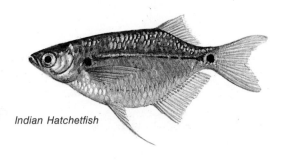

Indian Hatchetfish

J

JACK DEMPSEY (*Cichlasoma biocellatum* or *C. ostofasciatum*): Popularly named for its unrestrained pugnacity and its slight facial resemblance to the blue-jowled former heavyweight champion, this good-sized burly cichlid long has been one of the most popular of the egg-layers. Prized for its dark, blue-speckled beauty, its longevity, readiness to breed, and gentleness with its young, it is marked with two ocellated spots, one in the center of its body, the other at the caudal base. *Habitat:* Northern Brazil. *Diet:* Coarsely chopped meaty foods. NOTE: Should not be kept with smaller fish or fragile plants.

JACKNIFE FISH: *see* RIBBON FISH.

JANUARY TETRA (*Hemigrammus hyanuary*): a small, peaceable, relatively colorless tetra with a silver-white belly, greenish back and sides, a thin golden lateral stripe, and a dark spot on the caudal fin. Best kept in schools. *Habitat:* Colombia. *Diet:* Varied.

JAPANESE COLORED CARP: *see* KOI.

JAPANESE WEATHERFISH (*Misgurnus anguillicaudatus*):

Japanese Weatherfish

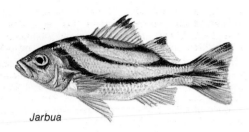

Jarbua

This good-sized eellike manic-depressive is given to alternating bouts of sudden erratic movement and long periods of immobility during which it lies buried up to its eyes in sand or gravel. A light, mottled gray in color, it lacks the articulated spiny armor below the eye characteristic of most similar loaches. *Habitat:* Japan, China. *Diet:* Varied, with live worms and tank detritus preferred.

JARBUA or **TARGET FISH** (*Therapon jarbua*): Basically a marine fish, but capable of adapting to fresh water, this large, silvery creature is marked with a series of dark concentric arcs resembling a section of a marksman's target. The temperament of this spiny-rayed fish is a matter of considerable debate, some observers having found it peaceable and others quarrelsome. In any case, it is not often exported from its native haunts, possibly because it is prized there as a food fish. *Habitat:* Coastal East Africa, throughout southern Asia, northern Australian littoral, with greatest prevalence in India, around the mouth of the Ganges. *Diet:* Extremely varied, with quantity the prime consideration. NOTE: Thrives best in slightly salt water.

JAVA KILLIE or **JAVANESE RICE FISH** (*Oryzias javanicus*): a smaller, stockier, more translucent version of the MEDAKA (*O. latipes*), it is a more finicky eater than its Japanese relative and usually will not bother with food that has fallen to the bottom of the tank. *Habitat:* Java, Malay Peninsula. *Diet:* Varied, with small live foods much preferred.

JAVANESE LOACH (*Acanthophthalmus javanicus*): This slender, silver-bodied creature bears a short vertical black bar at the base of the caudal fin. An excellent scavenger, it can penetrate almost inaccessible crevices and recesses. *Habitat:* Java, Sumatra. *Diet:* Small live worms, tank detritus.

JAVANESE RICE FISH: *see* JAVA KILLIE.

JAWFISH: any of several marine fishes of the family OPISTHOGNATHIDAE, of which the yellowhead, marbled, and pearly jawfish are among the most popular with aquarists, largely because of their propensity for "dancing" on their tails, and because of the expressiveness of their faces.

JELLYBEAN TETRA (*Ladigesia roloffi*): a refulgent red-orange little fish with black-tipped dorsal and caudal fins, it is fast, active, and requires a covered tank. *Habitat:* West Africa. *Diet:* Varied, with small live foods preferred.

JELLYFISH: any of numerous marine coelenterates of the class Scyphozoa, typically bell shaped, gelatinous, colorless, and tentacled. The young of some smaller species are introduced into saltwater community tanks by some aquarists as novelties.

JEWEL CICHLID or **RED CICHLID** (*Hemichromis bimaculatus*): Although physically attractive, especially during the breeding period when its blue-spotted, yellow-green body turns a bright ruby-red, this good-sized cichlid has a disagreeable personality in no way offset by its talent for uprooting plants. Among the species' generally unpleasant characteristics is the male's tendency to wreak murderous vengeance on females imprudent enough to spurn his advances. *Habitat:* Widespread throughout Africa. *Diet:* Live or chopped meaty foods.

JEWEL FISH (*Microspathodon chrysyrus*): One of the most spectacular of the generally breathtaking marine fishes, this small demoiselle is of a velvety blue-black color patterned with tiny lozenges of a lighter, luminous blue. With age and increasing size, the fish's tail turns a fiery orange while its body gradually loses its markings. In its natural habitat it is happiest and at its most secure in close proximity to fire coral, which often is deadly poisonous to other creatures, humans included. *Habitat:* Offshore Florida waters adjacent to the Gulf Stream. *Diet:* Varied, with most standard aquarium foods enthusiastically accepted.

JULIE (*Julidochromis ornatus*): Unfortunately, this strikingly beau-

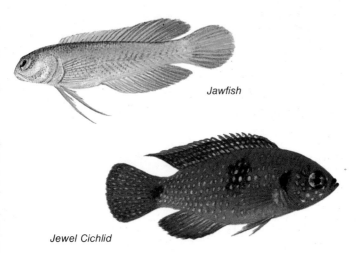

Jawfish

Jewel Cichlid

Jewel Fish

tiful cichlid requires water of an alkalinity far too high for most tropical fish. Vivid yellow and marked with three dark brown horizontal stripes extending almost the full length of its slender body, it is a fussy eater and rarely has reproduced its kind in captivity. *Habitat:* Lake Tanganyika, Africa. *Diet:* Unpredictable, with tubifex worms least likely to be rejected.

JUMPING CHARACIN or **SPRAYING CHARACIN** or **SPLASH TETRA** (*Copeina arnoldi* or *Pyrrhulina filamentosa*): a medium-sized, attractive characin,

it is most interesting for its unique spawning ritual, which involves acrobatics to rival those of a trapeze act. In captivity the male drives the female literally "up the wall," as both leap from the water, their fins interlocked, to adhere briefly to the side of a pane of frosted glass (a substitute for the low-hanging leaves of their natural habitat) against which the eggs are deposited. Brown with a yellowish belly, the male is somewhat larger than its mate. *Habitat:* Amazon River region. *Diet:* Varied, with small live foods preferred.

JURUPARI: *see* DEMON FISH.

Jumping Characin

110

KATANGA LAMPEYE (*Aplocheilichthys katangae*): a handsomely marked, little yellow cyprinodont with a dark zigzag line laterally transversing its body. Best kept in schools and away from larger predators. *Habitat:* Vicinity of Katanga, Congo. *Diet:* Small live foods.

KEYHOLE CICHLID (*Aequidens maroni*): One of the best behaved and most peaceable of the cichlids, this handsome fish is smaller than many of its cousins and far less destructive of aquatic plants. Ranging in its basic ground color from creamy tan to light brown, it is marked by an irregular vertical band running through the eye and, more distinctively, a keyhole-shaped band above the leading edge of the anal fin. Quick to breed, it is like most cichlids a very responsible parent. *Habitat:* British Guiana, Surinam. *Diet:* Small live foods.

KILLIFISH: any of some 200 known species of small, usually creek-dwelling fishes of the family CYPRINODONTIDAE, the egg-laying tooth-carps, which are related to the GAMBUSINOS, but lack the

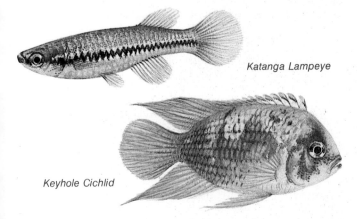

Katanga Lampeye

Keyhole Cichlid

Kissing Gourami

Koi

characteristic male gonopodium of the latter.

KISSING GOURAMI (*Helostoma rudolfi*): Just why a pair of these good-sized pale pink anabantids will swim toward each other, pucker their thick lips, and "kiss" has long been a subject of conjecture. Whatever the reason, the spectacle is amusing and has made the fish extremely popular with aquarists, even though it demands several feedings daily. Well behaved in community tanks and easily bred, it requires fairly warm water. *Habitat:* Southeast Asia, Malay Archipelago. *Diet:* Varied, with algae and dried floating foods, especially herbaceous matter, preferred.

KLAUSEWITZ' DWARF CICHLID (*Apistogramma klausewitzi*): a small, narrow-headed, relatively peaceable brownish-green species of which the male is

somewhat larger than its mate and distinguishable by the irregular shape of its dorsal fin. *Habitat:* Central Amazon region. *Diet:* Small live or chopped meaty foods.

KNIFE FISH: the popular name for the so-called gymnotid eels (family Gymnotidae), which are not true eels but are closely related to the characins. Characteristically, they lack dorsal and caudal fins and swim backward or forward by rippling their elongated anal fins.

KNIGHT GOBY (*Gobius sadanundio*): A nondescript but popular goby bearing irregular markings on its gray-brown body, it prefers brackish water and should be kept only with very small tankmates. *Habitat:* South Asia from the Malay Archipelago to the Philippines. *Diet:* Live foods in quantity.

KOI or **JAPANESE COLORED CARP:** a Japanese-bred decorative hybrid produced by crossing two European carps, *Carassius auratus gibelo* and *C. carassius*. Prized for its colorful calico markings and large size, it is particularly suited to outdoor garden display and will take almost any foods.

KORAN or **KORAN ANGELFISH** (*Pomacantus semicirculatus*): Named for its cursive markings, which are said to resemble characters from the Arabic, this striking black, white and blue-purple marine fish's delicate constitution make it an unsuitable subject for inexperienced saltwater aquarists. The name "Koran" is sometimes improperly used to designate the emperor angel fish. *Habitat:* Indo-Pacific region. *Diet:* Small live foods supplemented with ground shrimp and herbaceous matter.

KUHLII LOACH: *see* COOLIE LOACH.

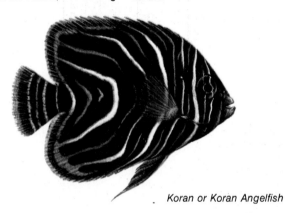

Koran or Koran Angelfish

L

LABARRE'S APHYOSEMION
(*Aphyosemion labarrei*): The male of this small, slender killifish species, with its pale blue body spotted and horizontally striped in blood red, is much the handsomer of the sexes. Docile and well adapted to community life, but an incorrigible jumper whose tank must be kept covered. *Habitat:* Lower Congo River basin. *Diet:* Small live foods much preferred.

LABRIDAE: the taxonomic family embracing the wrasses, one of the largest groups of temperate and tropical marine fishes, whose members range in size from some 3 inches up to 10 feet or more, are generally elongated, often thick-lipped and equipped with strong teeth, and usually are highly colored or vividly marked.

LABYRINTH FISHES: *see* ANABANTIDAE.

LABYRINTH ORGAN: the respiratory system unique to members of family Anabantidae, consisting of a concentric arrangement of bony plates, an enlarged gill cavity, and within the latter a vascular membrane which allows the fish to retain and breathe air.

LADIGES' GAUCHO (*Cynopoecilus ladigesi*): a small, red-barred, green fish with green eyes. Quite handsomely marked in the fin areas, it is an extremely prolific egg-burier. *Habitat:* Minas Gerais State, Brazil. *Diet:* Small live foods.

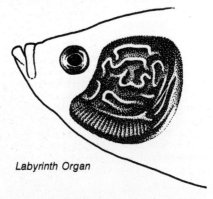

Labyrinth Organ

Ladiges' Gaucho

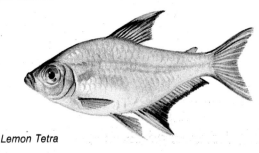

Lemon Tetra

LAMP-EYE: (1) (*Aplocheilichthys macrophthalmus* or *Micropanchax macrophthalmus*): a small, slender killifish whose metallic green eyes seem to glow with interior illumination under favorable top-lighting. Peaceable, but should not be kept with predatory species. *Habitat:* Nigeria. *Diet:* Small live and dried foods. (2) Any of several related species (and some unrelated marine species) with similarly luminous eyes.

LEAF FISH (*Monocirrhus polyacanthus*): Camouflaged to resemble a floating fallen leaf, this curious nandid's most peculiar characteristic is its ability seemingly to turn the lining of its mouth inside-out while indulging in its frequent, cavernous yawns. *Habitat:* Tropical South America. *Diet:* Small live fish exclusively.

LEERI: *see* PEARL GOURAMI.

LEMON CICHLID (*Lamprologus leleupi*): Medium-sized, slender, blue-eyed, and yellow-bodied, this is perhaps the least bellicose of the cichlids and adapts well to community tanks provided with adequate shelter. *Habitat:* Lake Tanganyika, Africa. *Diet:* Live foods.

LEMON TETRA (*Hyphessobrycon pulchripinnis*): Except for its red-rimmed eye and the vivid yellow of its shapely anal fin, this popular characin is relatively colorless, but lively in its movements. Well-behaved in community tanks if kept in small schools, it breeds with some difficulty and is prone to cannibalize its eggs. *Habitat:* Northern Brazil. *Diet:* Varied, with small live foods preferred.

LEOPARD CATFISH or **LEOPARD CORYDORAS** (*Corydoras julii*): a small, hardy, handsomely spotted armored catfish, more or

115

Leopard Danio

Lionhead Goldfish

less typical in shape and behavior of the *Corydoras* generally. *Habitat:* Lower Amazon River region. *Diet:* Varied and supplemented with scavenged matter.

LEOPARD DANIO (*Brachydanio frankei*): Resembling a miniature trout, this peaceable, active creature thrives in community tanks if kept in small schools. *Habitat:* India. *Diet:* Varied.

LIONFISH or **TURKEYFISH** or **COBRA FISH** (*Pterois volitans*): By all odds the most spectacular of the marine aquarium fishes, this venomous member of family Scorpaenidae (the scorpion fishes) is large, magnificently marked with rust-red and white bands, and equipped with a startling array of quill-like fins and spines which it waves languidly when at rest and spreads alarmingly when aroused. Although generally hardy, the lionfish is sensitive to, and can be blinded by, overexposure to strong light. Otherwise, it is easily kept, even by beginners, but should be treated with circumspection, for its poisonous spines can inflict painful and even quite serious wounds. While it can be kept in community aquaria, it is shown to best advantage (and maintains its health and composure better) in isolation. *Habitat:* Tropical Indo-Pacific waters. *Diet:* Small live fish.

LIONHEAD CICHLID (*Steatocranus casuarius*): a rather small, dull-gray, fairly peaceable cichlid distinguished by a huge rounded protuberance on the adult male's head. *Habitat:* Stanley Pool, Africa. *Diet:* Live and coarsely chopped meaty foods, with frozen foods taken reluctantly.

LIONHEAD GOLDFISH: a variety of eggfish, in turn a variety of goldfish (*Carassius auratus*), characterized by the irregular warty growths covering its usually red head.

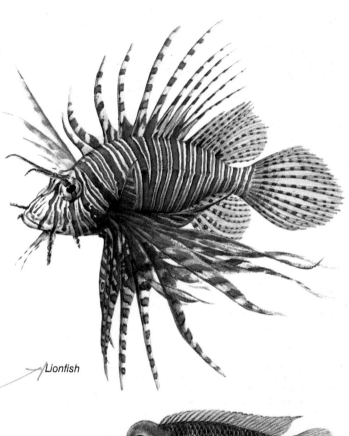

Lionfish

Lionhead Cichlid

LIPSTICK LEPORINUS (*Leporinus arcus*): a charcacin, smaller but otherwise similar in behavior and appearance, except for its markedly red lips and fins, to the striped leporinus (*L. striatus*). *Habitat:* Northern South America. *Diet:* Small live and frozen foods, herbaceous matter.

LIVE-BEARER: *see* POECILIIDAE.

LOACH: Any member of the family COBITIDAE.

LONGFIN BARB (*Capoeta arulius*): a large but otherwise typical barb, its distinguishing characteris-

117

tic is the attenuation of the dorsal fin in the adult male. Silver-gray and tinged with red, it is well behaved and active. *Habitat:* India. *Diet:* Varied; live foods preferred.

LONG-FINNED BATFISH: *see* ORANGE-RINGED BATFISH.

LONGNOSE AUSTRALIAN BUTTERFLY: *see* COPPERBAND BUTTERFLY FISH).

LONGNOSED FILEFISH: *see* ORANGE-SPOTTED FILEFISH.

LOOKDOWN (*Selene vomer*): This black-banded yellow marine fish grows to a foot in length and is characterized by the peculiar downward slant of its head. *Habitat:* Western Atlantic waters from New England to Brazil. *Diet:* Chopped crustaceans, depending on the size of the fish.

LORETO TETRA (*Hyphessobrycon peruvianus*): This small, shy, attractive characin is marked with a bold black stripe that runs most of the length of its body, dividing the olive-brown of the fish's back from its gray belly. The caudal fin is a deep red. *Habitat:* Peruvian

reaches of the Amazon River. *Diet:* Varied, with small live foods preferred.

LORICARIIDAE: the taxonomic family comprising the various spiny armored catfishes, all native to the New World and characteristically covered with rough bony plates and equipped with a disk-shaped mouth on the underside of the head. The SUCKER CATFISH is a typical species.

LUNGFISH: any of several members of the family Lepidosirenidae, distinguished by their ability to breathe air while estivating in a mud cocoon or shallow stagnant pool during dry seasons. Apparently descended from creatures closely related to the ancestors of the earliest amphibians, they are found in Africa, South America, and Australia, are eel-like in shape, and quite large. While generally sluggish, they are capable of inflicting severe bites. Unsuitable for community aquaria, most species thrive in captivity on a diet of live fish and earthworms, fresh meat, and live snails and mussels.

Loreto Tetra

Lyretail

LUTJANIDAE: the taxonomic family made up of the numerous perch-like, largely nocturnal marine fishes commonly called snappers and equipped with large canine teeth for grasping their prey. Much prized as food fishes, snappers also are commonly to be found in home aquaria.

LYRETAIL or **LYRETAILED PANCHAX** (*Aphyosemion aus-trale*): one of the most beautiful and most popular of the killifishes, the male of the species is marked with carmine spots on a brown ground and distinguished by the graceful attenuation of its dorsal, anal, and caudal fins. Peaceable and rather shy, it should not be exposed to fin-nipping species. *Habitat:* Cape Lopez vicinity, eastern equatorial Africa. *Diet:* Small live foods.

M

MALAPTERURIDAE: the taxonomic family comprising a single species, the ELECTRIC CATFISH (*Malapterurus electricus*).

MALAYAN ANGEL or **FINGERFISH** or **MONO** (*Monodactylus argenteus*): This handsome creature, with its silvery body and yellow-tipped fins, is one of the very few marine fish that can be kept in a freshwater aquarium with no apparent ill effects. Rather shy and easily upset, it is best kept in schools or, in community tanks, with species of a similar nature. *Habitat:* Indian Ocean. *Diet:* Brine shrimp, chopped fresh shrimp and earthworms, lean meats, all laced occasionally with paprika.

MALAYAN PUFFER: *see* COMMON PUFFER FISH.

MAN-OF-WAR FISH (*Nomeus gronovii*): a small silver-and-blue marine fish that rarely thrives in

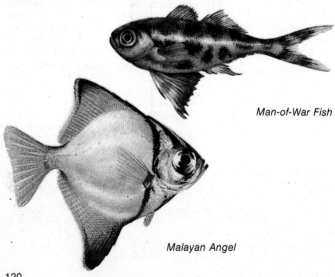

Man-of-War Fish

Malayan Angel

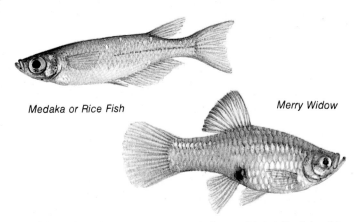

Medaka or Rice Fish

Merry Widow

captivity and is of interest chiefly for its unique ability to dwell safely within the ambit of the Portuguese man-of-war, a lethally venomous jellyfish. *Habitat:* Tropical waters throughout the world. *Diet:* Zooplankton and similar foods, small live fish, small crustaceans.

MARBLED CICHLID: see OSCAR.

MARBLED GOBY (*Oxyeleotris marmoratus*): This extremely large, big-mouthed goby is a voracious predator and altogether unsuitable for life in a community tank. Growing to a length of nearly a yard in its natural habitat, it bears mottled ivory markings on a variegated brown ground and, in nature, lies in wait for its prey on stream bottoms. *Habitat:* Malay Peninsula. *Diet:* Live fish, earthworms, fresh shrimp.

MEDAKA or **RICE FISH** (*Oryzias latipes*): This small, big-eyed golden killifish bears no distinctive markings, but is popular because of its great durability, its adaptability to community aquaria, its ability to withstand extreme temperature variations, and its willingness to

eat whatever it is fed. Easily bred, it spawns in an unusual manner, with the female first dangling clusters of eggs beneath her vent and then, after fertilization, transferring them to aquarium plants. *Habitat:* Japan, Korea, northeastern China. *Diet:* Omnivorous.

MERMAN'S SHAVING BRUSH (*Penicillus capitatus*): a small marine plant with an asparaguslike stalk and bushy top. Popular as a "hitching post" for seahorses.

MERRY WIDOW (*Phallichthys amates*): Once quite a popular aquarium fish, this diminutive live-bearer (the female, at 2 inches, is twice the size of her mate) gradually fell into obscurity as more colorful gambusinos appeared on the commercial market. Olive-brown or greenish-yellow with pale blue glints, it lives well with other species but tends to cannibalize its young. Its popular name derives from the black edging on the male's prominent dorsal fin. *Habitat:* West coast of Central America. *Diet:* Varied, with a preference for algae.

MEXICAN SWORDTAIL (*Xiphophorus montezumae*): Despite its popular name, this peaceable, rather nondescript gray-brown live-bearer hardly qualifies as a swordtail except technically, there being only a rudimentary attenuation of the lower rays of the male's caudal fin. About average in size for a gambusino, both sexes are marked with a dark zigzag line extending from behind the eye to the base of the tail. *Habitat:* Eastern Mexico. *Diet:* Omnivorous.

MEYERS' LAMPEYE: see HUMMINGBIRD FISH.

MINNOW: (1) *Phoxinus p.*, the common European cold-water cyprinid collected by some aquarists and fed by others to larger, more exotic tropical fish. *Habitat:* Widespread throughout the temperate zones. *Diet:* Small live foods. (2) The common designation for numerous killifish species.

MOCHOKIDAE: The taxonomic family comprised of a small number of tropical African catfishes, most of them bearing branched barbels on the lower lip and many of them given to swimming upside-down.

MOLLY: Any of several extremely popular *Mollienesia* of family Poeciliidae (the live-bearing tooth carps or gambusinos), of which the commonest is *M. sphenops* (see SPHENOPS).

MONACANTHIDAE: the taxonomic family embracing the various marine filefishes, close relatives of the triggerfishes, but distinguished from them by their less sophisticated dorsal finnage and their lack of bony body covering.

MONO: see MALAYAN ANGEL.

MONODACTYLIDAE: the taxonomic family consisting of the moonfishes—small, silvery estuarial fishes such as the MALAYAN ANGEL or Mono (*Monodactylus argenteus*), most of which thrive equally well in marine or freshwater aquaria.

MOONFISH: see PLATY.

MOORISH IDOL (*Zanclus cornutus* or *Z. canescens*): Breathtakingly beautiful but extremely fragile, this silvery, arrowhead-shaped creature is marked with three broad, velvety-black vertical bands, a black-outlined chrome yellow saddle on its snout, and a lemon-yellow area in the space between its attenuated dorsal and anal fins and its rather blunt tail. One of the most imposing of the marine tropicals, it is not recommended to the neophyte aquarist. *Habitat:* Tropical Pacific waters from Hawaii westward. *Diet:* Varied, with a mixture of ground shrimp and herbaceous matter taken most readily, and bloodworms, brine shrimp, and tubifex taken more reluctantly. NOTE: Food preferences vary greatly between one individual and another.

MORAY: any of various marine eels known for their ferociousness, fearlessness, and ability to inflict painful, often dangerous bites, *e.g.*, the black-edge moray (*Gymnothorax nigromarginatus*), some of which are kept by saltwater aquarists with a taste for the unusual. Hardy and largely nocturnal, they are quite ingenious escape artists and should be kept in maximum-security tanks. *Habitat:*

Moorish Idol

Widespread throughout temperate and tropical waters. *Diet:* Shrimp, live fish, chopped sea scallops.

MORMYRIDAE: the taxonomic family comprising the so-called elephant fishes of tropical Africa, many of which are characterized by inordinately large brains, trunk-like snouts, and the ability to discharge a weak electric current.

MOSAIC GOURAMI: *see* PEARL GOURAMI.

MOSQUITO FISH: the common name applied to a variety of tropical fishes, including *Gambusia afinis a., G. afinis holbooki, Heterandria formosa,* and *Glaridichthys falcatus*.

MOSQUITO LARVAE: the newly hatched, still wingless young of various common mosquitoes, popular with aquarists as a live food for tropical fish.

MOUTHBREEDERS or **MOUTH-BROODERS:** any of various

Mouthbreeders

123

fishes, chiefly cichlids of the genus *Tilapia*, that carry their fertilized eggs in either or both parents' mouths until they have hatched and, in some cases, continue to carry the fry in the same manner.

MOZAMBIQUE CICHLID or **MOZAMBIQUE TILAPIA** (*Tilapia mossambica*): A typical MOUTH-BREEDER, this good-sized creature, eaten as a food fish in Africa, is generally a velvety greenish-black except at breeding time, when the male's lower jaw turns white and the tip of the yellow-green caudal fin takes on a red flush. *Habitat:* East Africa. *Diet:* Omnivorous. NOTE: Generally well behaved, but should not be kept with much smaller fishes.

MUDFISH: *see* BOWFIN.

MUDSKIPPER (*Periopthalmus barbarus*): In its natural habitat this intriguing creature lives an amphibious life on the tidal mud flats of the Indo-Australian Archipelago. Equipped with froglike protuberant eyes and a highly developed musculature that enables it to rise, "walk," and even skip on its pectoral fins, it spends much of its time basking contentedly on the mud and acting very unlike the proverbial "fish out of water." Greenish-brown with light blue mottlings and with sharply defined blue-and-white stripes on its two dorsal fins, the mudskipper requires a very warm, enclosed aquarium, shallow brackish water and a rising, moist slope to climb upon. *Habitat:* Tropical littoral from India to East Africa, Polynesia, Australia. *Diet:* Live insects, worms, chopped shrimp.

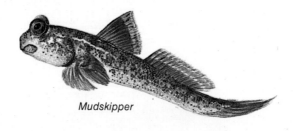

Mudskipper

MULLIDAE: the taxonomic family made up of some 50 species of marine goatfishes, most of which are indigenous to tropical sea beds, many of which are red in color and all of which are distinguishable by the long barbels with thich they scour bottom sands for food.

MURAENIDAE: the taxonomic family comprising the marine moray eels, similar to the conger eels (family CONGRIDAE), but lacking pectoral fins.

MYERS' CATFISH (*Corydoras myersi*): Otherwise similar to such corydoras species as the AENEUS CATFISH, it is distinguished by the vivid red-and-green coloration of its early youth. *Habitat:* Northwestern Brazil. *Diet:* Varied.

MYERS' LAMPEYE: *see* HUMMINGBIRD FISH.

N

NANDIDAE: the largest taxonomic family of spiny-rayed freshwater fishes, it comprises such well-known species as the BADIS (*Badis badis*) and the AFRICAN LEAF FISH (*Polycentropsis abbreviata*).

NATTERER'S PIRAHNA or **RED-BELLIED PIRAHNA** (*Serrasalmo nattereri*): A large, ferocious predator, this commonest of the piranhas has a blue-gray body flushed with red along its underside from beneath the lower lip to the end of the anal fin. *Habitat:* Orinoco and Amazon basins. *Diet:* Small live fish, raw food fish, meaty foods. NOTE: Must be isolated.

NAUPLII: The newly hatched young of the BRINE SHRIMP.

NEON DISEASE or **PLISTOPHORA:** *see* DISEASES OF TROPICAL FISH.

NEON GOBY (*Lactinius oceanops* or *Gobiosoma o.*): Furnished with a few large shells or other hiding places, this small, beautiful

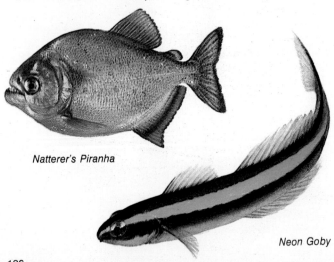

Natterer's Piranha

Neon Goby

blue marine fish is easily bred. It makes an extremely useful addition to the community aquarium, where it will keep other species free of most parasites. *Habitat:* Florida Keys, West Indian waters. *Diet:* Dried foods, small live foods, foraged parasites.

NEON TETRA (*Hyphessobrycon innesi*): One of the most beautiful and best-known of the freshwater tropicals, this small, slender, peaceable characin is shown to best advantage in schools and against dark backgrounds, with lighting arranged to heighten the rich glow of its blue, green, and red coloration. Difficult to breed. *Habitat:* Amazon River region near the Brazilian-Peruvian border. *Diet:* Fine dried or very small live foods.

NUDIBRANCH: any of numerous, often highly colored shell-less gas-tropod mollusks of the taxonomic suborder Nudibranchiata, commonly called "sea slugs," and prized by marine aquarists as scavengers of algae.

NURSE SHARK (*Ginglymostoma cirratum*): One of the smaller of the true sharks and one of the most easily tamed, this gray-brown creature (spotted when young) will thrive in the home marine aquarium (at least, until it outgrows its tank), but should be handled with care. *Habitat:* Western Atlantic waters. *Diet:* Fresh shrimp, scallops, small live fish, crabs.

NURSE TETRA (*Alestes nurse*): A very large, active, relatively colorless characin, it is somewhat shy and will school with its own species in a community aquarium. *Habitat:* Tropical Africa. *Diet:* Large live foods, chopped earthworms, coarse meaty foods.

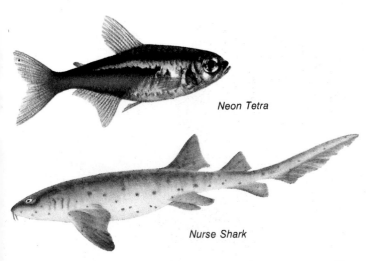

Neon Tetra

Nurse Shark

OCELLATED DWARF RAS-BORA: *see* EXCLAMATION-POINT RASBORA.

OCELLUS: a spot or marking resembling an eye and found on various fauna, including many tropical fish. In some cases, this protective device is rudimentary, but it is often fully detailed and quite convincingly realistic.

OCTOPUS: any of numerous eight-armed dibranchiate cephalopods, some smaller species of which occasionally are dept as curiosities, but with difficulty, by marine aquarists.

OODINIUM: *see* DISEASES OF TROPICAL FISH.

OPISTHOGNATHIDAE: the taxonomic family comprising the various marine JAWFISH, so called for their disproportionately large jaws. Characteristically builders of burrows, they normally hover in a vertical position, "standing" or "dancing" on their tails, and disappear tail-first into their burrows when threatened.

ORANGE CHROMIDE or **ORANGE CICHLID** (*Etroplus maculatus*): One of the few known Asiatic cichlids, this rather small, attractive species is more peaceable than most of its South American relatives and better suited to community tanks. Individual specimens vary in body color from pale yellow to burnt orange, but invariably bear a dark spot in the middle of the body. *Habitat:* India, Sri Lanka. *Diet:* Live and frozen foods.

Orange Chromide or Orange Cichlid

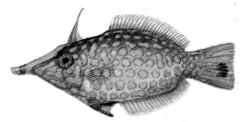

Orange-Spotted Filefish

Oscar or Marbled Cichlid

ORANGE-RINGED BATFISH or **LONG-FINNED BATFISH** (*Platax pinnatus*). At its best, before its color begins to fade with maturity, this is one of the most breathtakingly beautiful of all marine fishes. Large and uncommonly graceful, it is jet black when young, with a bright orange band more or less completely outlining its silhouette. *Habitat:* Western Pacific and India Oceans. *Diet:* Omnivorous, with small live fish preferred.

ORANGE-SPOTTED FILEFISH or **LONGNOSED FILEFISH** (*Oxymonacanthus longirostris*): This rather small green-bodied creature is one of the most vividly colored of the marine FILEFISHES, with regular rows of orange spots extending laterally from just behind the snout to the caudal base. *Habitat:* Indo-Pacific region. *Diet:* Varied, with crustaceans and herbaceous matter frequently required.

ORNATE CTENOPOMA (*Ctenopoma ansorgei*): Well behaved in large community aquaria, except with creatures smaller than itself, this perpetually hungry labyrinth fish bears several blue-green vertical bands on its blue body and grows to a length of about 2 ¾ inches. *Habitat:* Tropical West Africa. *Diet:* Unwanted small fish and other live foods, chopped earthworms, coarse meaty foods.

OSCAR or **MARBLED CICHLID** (*Astronotus ocellatus*): One of the handsomest, largest and least

129

OSTEOGLOSSIDAE: The taxonomic family comprising the five extant species of the so-called bony-tongued fishes that originated during the Jurassic era, all of which are large, sharp-toothed, and bear prominent scales. The best known of the five is the AROWANA (*Osteoglossum bicirrhosum*).

OSTRACIIDAE: The taxonomic family comprising the various, often poisonous, marine fishes known as truckfishes, boxfishes, or cowfishes and characterized by a bony protective carapace furnished with openings through which the major external organs protrude.

OXYGEN: *see* AQUARIUM CARE AND MANAGEMENT.

characteristic of the cichlids, this intelligent creature bears mottlings on its body that may range from a gray-green to a dark chocolate-brown and carries a vivid red ocellus, at the base of the tail. Atypically, its scales are hardly visible, giving the oscar's skin a suedelike appearance that has inspired some hobbyists to dub the fish "velvet cichlid." Altogether unsuited to community aquaria except when very young, it is best kept in pairs, and spawns by laying strings of tiny eggs in intricate patterns on the tank bottom. *Habitat:* The Guianas, Venezuela, the Amazon basin to the Paraguayan border. *Diet:* Unwanted live fish, chunky raw beef organs, coarsely cut food fish.

P

PACIFIC BLUE ANGELFISH: *see* BLUE ANGELFISH.

PANCHAX: (1) any of several usually brightly colored killifishes of the genus *Aplocheilus* and related genera; (2) more particularly, *Aplocheilus panchax,* an easily bred, long-popular aquarium fish bearing red and yellow markings on an olive-green ground. Peaceable and well behaved in community tanks. *Habitat:* India, southeast Asia. *Diet:* Varied, with small live foods preferred.

PANTODONTIDAE: the taxonomic family comprising a single species, the BUTTERFLY FISH (*Pantodon buchholzi*).

PARADISE FISH (*Macropodus opercularis*): This hardy creature generally is considered the earliest tropical aquarium fish imported into Europe, having been introduced in Paris in 1868. Rather small for an anabantid, it has a body alternately banded in vivid tones of red and blue, but the fish's greediness and nasty disposition offsets its undeniable beauty and it remains unpopular with community aquarists. *Habitat:* Southern China, Taiwan. *Diet:* Varied, with frequent feedings indicated.

PARALYTIC SHOCK: *see* DISEASES OF TROPICAL FISH.

PARASITES: *see* DISEASES OF TROPICAL FISH.

PARROT FISH: any of the large, colorful marine species belonging to family *Scaridae,* having fused teeth of a beaklike appearance, and given to constructing sleeping cocoons of mucous.

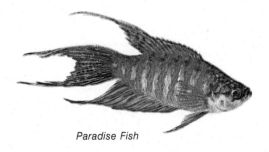

Paradise Fish

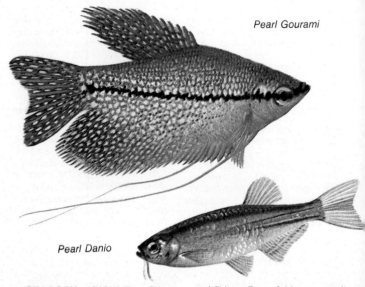

Pearl Gourami

Pearl Danio

PEACOCK CICHLID (*Tilapia sparrmani*): This large olive-brown African cichlid's dorsal fin is flecked with red-tipped blues and bears a curious ocelluslike mark at its base. The species, which does not adapt to community tanks, should not be confused with mouthbreeders bearing the generic designation *Tilapia*, or with the Oscar (*Astronotus ocellatus*), also called peacock cichlid by some fanciers. *Habitat:* Southwest and south central Africa. *Diet:* Live foods, coarse meaty foods, unwanted small fish.

PEARL DANIO (*Brachydanio albolineatus*): Under good illumination, especially natural sunlight, this medium-sized fish, with its shimmering nacreous coloration, is transformed from a relatively drab creature to one of the most dazzling of the better-known tropical fishes. Peaceful in community tanks, active, not at all finicky about its diet, and quick to breed, it is deservedly popular, especially with beginning aquarists. *Habitat:* India, Burma, Malay Archipelago. *Diet:* Varied, with small live foods taken enthusiastically.

PEARL GOURAMI or **MOSAIC GOURAMI** or **LEERI** (*Trichogaster leeri*): Silvery with a violet sheen and spangled with pearllike spots, this medium-sized bubblenest builder bears a dark horizontal stripe, running through the eye, from its snout to the base of the tail. Considered by many enthusiasts to be the most beautiful of the gouramis, it is peaceful to the point of timidity and adapts well to community aquaria. *Habitat:* Thailand, Malay Peninsula, Malay Archipelago. *Diet:* Dried foods regularly, with occasional live feedings.

PEMPHERIDAE: the taxonomic family comprising the marine sweepers, relatively small, nocturnal reef-dwellers characterized by their deep-bellied tapering bodies, small centrally-positioned dorsal fin, elongated anal fin, and large eyes.

PERUVIAN DWARF CICHLID (*Apistogramma ambloplitoides*): One of the least colorful of the cichlids, this relatively short-bodied, rather peaceful creature is brownish in color with a faint violet sheen and bears a series of indistinct vertical bands. *Habitat:* Peru. *Diet:* Live or fresh meaty foods, frozen foods taken less enthusiastically.

PERUVIAN LONGFIN (*Pterolebias peruensis*): The male of this graceful killifish species is endowed with a large bannerlike tail, but his mate makes do with a rounded caudal fin of much more modest dimensions. Light brown with a series of darker vertical bars, both sexes bear light blue spots on the dorsal and anal fins.

Habitat: Eastern Peru. *Diet:* Varied live foods. NOTE: Should be bred in the same manner as other "annual" egg-buriers, *i.e.*, provided with a layer of peat moss in which to spawn.

pH: *see* WATER.

PHANTOM LARVAE: *see* GLASS LARVAE.

PHILIPPINE BUMBLEBEE (*Brachygobius aggregatus*): Similar to the bumblebeefish (*B. xanthozona*) except for a lack of sharp definition in its markings, it requires harder, warmer water. *Habitat:* Philippine Islands. *Diet:* Small live foods.

PIKE CICHLID (*Crenicichla lepidota*): This long-bodied, large-mouthed predator cannot safely be kept in a community tank. The fish has a generally gray- or greenish-brown body; the anal and caudal fins bear red shadings and gray dots. *Habitat:* Central South America. *Diet:* Unwanted fish and other live foods.

Peruvian Longfin

Pike Cichlid

Pipefish

PIKE TOP MINNOW or **PIKE LIVEBEARER** (*Belonesox belizanus*): The largest of the tropical live-bearers, this trap-jawed cannibal has as vicious a disposition as any predator in the world and can be trusted with nothing that moves. Grayish-green and black-spotted, the female of the species usually is larger than the male. *Habitat:* Southern Mexico and Central America. *Diet:* Large live foods exclusively.

PIMELODIDAE: the taxonomic family comprising various unarmored South American catfishes, usually bearing elongated barbels and well-defined dorsal fins.

PIPEFISH: (1) Any of several marine fishes related to the sea horse, typified by a similar snout and characterized by a slender elongated body, of which several species, such as *Corythoichthys albirostris*, are popular among saltwater aquarists. (2) Any of several related so-called freshwater fishes, actually native to brackish waters, such as the African freshwater pipefish (*Syngnathus pulchellus*), covered with bony plates and with the males, like male sea horses, equipped with a brood pouch. NOTE: All pipefishes, marine or "freshwater," must be fed live foods.

PIRANHA: any of a number of South American characins, of which members of the genera *Serrasalmus*, *Rooseveltiella*, and *Pygocentrus* are equipped with blunt, powerful jaws and unusually sharp teeth. Generally sizable and given to schooling in their native haunts, they have inspired much lurid and often wildly exaggerated description of their allegedly murderous propensities.

PISHUNA (*Aequidens tetramerus*): A more or less typical cichlid of about average size, this olive-backed, silver-bellied fish bears several indistinct vertical bands on its body and has been the subject of much nomenclatural confusion generated by its unusually extensive range. *Habitat:* From the Guianas southward to Rio de Janeiro. *Diet:* Small live and coarse meaty foods.

PLANKTON: collectively, the passively drifting or weakly swimming, usually minute life, animal and vegetable, to be found in bodies of water. One of the most nutritive of all food forms, it is collected in fine-mesh nets by many marine aquarists who feed it, live or frozen, to fry and smaller fish.

PLANTS, AQUATIC: Although their primary role has been purely an aesthetic one since the advent of the electric-powered aerator, aquarium plants continue to perform several useful functions: They serve as indicators of the aquarium's general health; they provide various supplements to the diets of fish, either directly or as hosts to a number of nutritious organisms; they offer security to weaker or timid fish; they serve as repositories for the eggs of spawning fish; they inhibit the excessive growth of algae. Kept free of parasites, protected from those fish that might nibble, strip, or uproot them, and provided with adequate light, most aquarium plants will thrive with little further care than an occasional pruning and the trimming away of unsightly dead leaves. As a general rule, it is more convenient and aesthetically pleasing to grow rooted aquatic plants—especially the taller varieties, toward the rear of the tank, where they serve as a sort of theatrical backdrop, both setting off and affording a clear view of the principal actors, the fish. Moreover, by restricting growth to the rear portion of the tank, the aquarist who fancies particularly destructive fish can protect his plants by interposing a pane of clear glass between the two. Wherever they are placed, however, rooted pants should be provided with enough compost (see AQUARIUM CARE AND MANAGEMENT) to anchor them firmly.

OVERLEAF: *A well-planted freshwater aquarium.*

Live plants used in aquarium help supply oxygen to the fish.

SOME POPULAR AQUARIUM PLANTS: Ornamental aquatic vegetation can be considered as belonging to either of two broad categories: rooted plants and floating plants. Rooted plants either grow entirely under water or, as is the case with bog plants, are rooted underwater but bear their leaves and flowers in the air. The overwhelming preponderance of both rooted and floating plants are flowering (although constant pruning of aquarium specimens inhibits or aborts the production of blossoms and seeds), but a number of popular species are nonflowering and reproduce by the dissemination of microscopic spores. A selection of the more popular aquarium plants follows:

Amazon Swordplant: The popular designation for the two best-known species of genus *Echinodorus*, all whose members are native to the Americas: (1) *E. paniculatus*, the broad-leaved relative of (2) *E. breripedicellatus*. Both are rooted, with loosely arranged bladelike leaves growing upward from the base of a central stem, and with propagation accomplished by the putting out of runners.

Cellophane Plant (*Echinodorus berteroi*): A graceful plant bearing heart-shaped leaves that often grow, with the blossoms, above the water level.

Pigmy Chain Swordplant (*E. tenellus*): Well suited to small shallow aquaria, this smallest of the popular members of genus *Echinodorus* grows to a height of only two inches or so.

Wavy Swordplant (*Echinodorus martii*): This splendid plant is

fully subaqueous, with long, tapering, ripple-edged leaves, and propagates by putting forth small plants from a submerged central flower stalk.

Corkscrew Vallisneria (*Vallisneria spiralis*): Commonly called "eel grasses," the members of genus *Vallisneria* are all grasslike plants that propagate by putting out runners. Corkscrew vallisneria proliferates rapidly in subdued light and will soon cover the aquarium floor if not thinned.

Common Eelgrass or **Italian Val** (*Vallisneria torta*): Very similar to corkscrew vallisneria, except that the leaves are straighter and have less tendency to spiral.

Sagittaria subulata: Bearing oval leaves at the ends of long graceful stems, and pale blue flowers, this is the most popular plant of genus *Sagittaria*. Very adaptable, it grows subaqueously or as a bog plant and propagation is accomplished for the most part by runners.

Cabomba (*Cabomba caroliniana*): One of several very similar fanworts, this is generally considered one of the most beautiful of all aquarium plants, but is difficult to control and should be avoided by neophytes. Fast-growing, with fine needlelike leaves, it is bright green when kept at relatively high temperatures, but takes on a purplish hue in cool water.

Cabomba aquatica: Similar to the above in its general structure, this handsome plant bears deep yellow blossoms.

Cabomba australis: Found in Argentina, Chile, and Uraguay, this plant has divided bright green leaves and white blossoms.

Water Milfoil (*Myriophyllum*): Any of several similar species of fine-leaved fernlike cool-water plants, these are particularly well suited to use in breeding tanks.

Cryptocoryne affinis or **C. haerteliana:** Native to the Malay Archipelago, this striking plant requires little light, grows to about a foot in height, and bears spearlike leaves with dark green surfaces and wine-red undersides.

Cryptocoryne willissii: Bearing long, wavy, tapering leaves with dark green upper surfaces and brown undersides, this is a rather variable plant with a frequently erratic growth pattern.

Cryptocoryne eiliata: Kept submerged, this quite large species puts forth long, slightly wavy swordlike leaves, but if allowed to grow as a bog plant, the leaves take on a much squatter heart-shaped silhouette. Its blossom is pale and pointed, with a reddish, fringed edge.

Madagascar Lace Plant (*Aponogeton fenestralis*): Fragile, relatively rare and hard to maintain, its finely veined semitransparent pale olive-green leaves make it one of the most hauntingly beautiful of the aquarium plants. It estivates periodically for several months at a stretch, during which time the plant seems to have died.

Aponogeton ulvaceus: Large and striking, with somewhat crinkly translucent leaves, this is an extremely fragile plant that tends to wax and wane with seasonal changes.

Water Hyacinth (*Eichornia crassipes*): A floating plant requiring plenty of natural light, it has curiously swollen leaf stems and bears a purple blossom.

Fairy Moss (*Azolla*): Any of several similarly constructed small floating plants bearing tight artichokelike clusters of leaves and tending to form a dense surface covering if not frequently thinned.

Najas: Closely resembling the herb tarragon, this rather fragile plant normally floats, but can be anchored to the aquarium bottom.

Crystalwort (*Riccia*): A very useful addition to breeding tanks, especially where live-bearers are concerned, this dense raftlike plant offers excellent cover for very young fry.

Salvinia auriculata: This fast-proliferating, nonflowering European floating plant bears double rows of circular, water-repellent leaves, each half of which is set at an incline angle to the other. Requires frequent thinning, but provides excellent refuge for fry.

Water Lettuce (*Pistia*): Also liked by fry, this thick-leaved, bluish plant looks very much like floating lettuce and, provided with good natural light, propagates itself rapidly by putting forth runners.

MARINE PLANTS: While saltwater aquaria are in most respects far more spectacular than even the most beautiful of freshwater tanks, their vegetation, most of it varieties of algae and all inclined to be scrubby, is no match for freshwater vegetation. Many marine fish like a bit of growing food, however, and mostly for that reason some saltwater aquarists plant their tanks.

OVERLEAF: *Some of the more popular types of aquatic plants.*

139

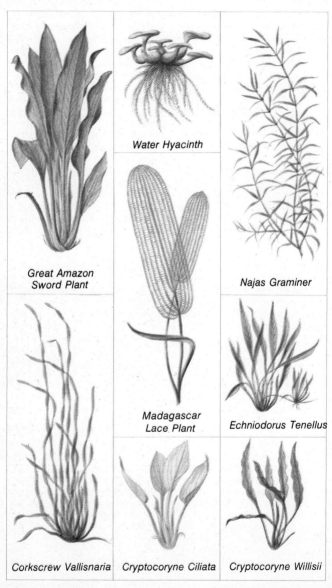

Great Amazon
Sword Plant

Water Hyacinth

Najas Graminer

Madagascar
Lace Plant

Echniodorus Tenellus

Corkscrew Vallisnaria

Cryptocoryne Ciliata

Cryptocoryne Willisii

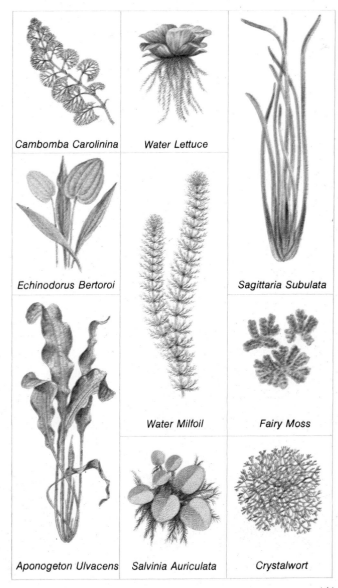

Cambomba Carolinina

Water Lettuce

Echinodorus Bertoroi

Water Milfoil

Sagittaria Subulata

Fairy Moss

Aponogeton Ulvacens

Salvinia Auriculata

Crystalwort

PLATACIDAE: the taxonomic family made up of the various Pacific and Atlantic BATFISHES, characterized by their elongated dorsal and anal fins, and much prized by marine aquarists.

PLATY or **MOONFISH** (*Xiphophorus maculatus*): This small, compact, extremely peaceful gambusino and the many hybrids that derive from it is one of the most easily kept and therefore most popular of freshwater tripical fish. It is a source of endless fascination for beginning aquarists and advanced geneticists alike. In the wild state, the platy most commonly tends toward a blue-green coloration, but selective breeding has produced such distinct forms as the blue, red, black, golden, and wagtail platies, along with the spotted platy and a near-infinitude of the so-called variegated platies. *Habitat:* Southern Mexico. *Diet:* Omnivorous.

PLISTOPHORA or **NEON DISEASE:** *see* DISEASES OF TROPICAL FISH.

POECILIIDAE: taxonomic family embracing the live-bearing Tooth Carps (gambusinos), or ovoviviparous fishes, which carry their eggs in the female's brood pouch, where they are fertilized by the male and where they remain until the young hatch and fully develop. In male live-bearers, puberty signals a metamorphosis in the anal fin of the male, which changes its shape and function. The resultant gonopodium, a kind of penis, henceforth serves as the conduit whereby the sperm is carried to the female's brood pouch. The platies, guppies, mollies, and swordtails

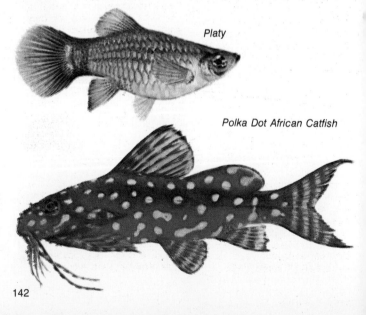

Platy

Polka Dot African Catfish

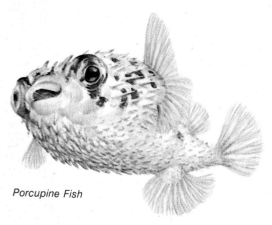

Porcupine Fish

are numbered among the better-known members of the family Poeciliidae.

POLKA DOT AFRICAN CATFISH (*Synodontis angelicus*): Blue-black, covered with ivory-white spots, and bearing four vertical white bands on its caudal fin, this large mochokid catfish is exceptionally attractive and well behaved around other species. *Habitat:* Tropical West Africa. *Diet:* Live worms, standard aquarium foods, algae.

POLYP: any of numerous marine organisms, such as coral, with a cylindrical body and tentacle-surrounded mouth opening, many varieties of which have been introduced into saltwater aquaria.

POMACANTHIDAE: the taxonomic family consisting of the marine angelfishes, which, with the BUTTERFLY FISHES, are among the most beautiful and popular of all saltwater creatures. Outstanding examples include the EMœ PEROR ANGELFISH (*Pomacanthus imperator*) and KORAN ANGELFISH (*P. semicirculatus*).

POMACENTRIDAE: the taxonomic family comprising the various damselfish or ANEMONE FISH: small marine species characterized by their tendency to seek the protection of intricate coral formations and the normally deadly ambit of the sea anemones. The BLUE DEMOISELLE (*Abudefduf caeruleus)* and the CLOWN ANEMONE (*Amphriprion percula*) are characteristic.

POMADASYIDAE: the taxonomic family comprising the grunts; snapperlike marine fishes characterized by their grunting sounds produced by the grinding of their teeth and amplified by their swim bladders.

POMPADOUR: *see* RED DISCUS.

POPEYE: *see* DISEASES OF TROPICAL FISH.

PORCUPINE FISH (*Diodon hystrix*): A large reef-dwelling marine puffer, or blowfish, with sharp erectile spines, this engaging creature is much enjoyed for its humorous, seemingly expressive aspect and for its puppylike actions. Well-behaved in community

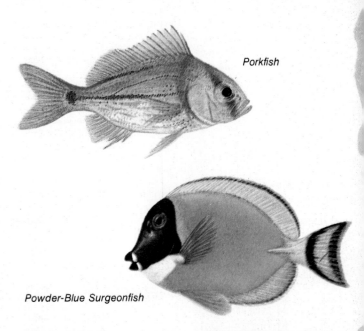

Porkfish

Powder-Blue Surgeonfish

aquaria except for a tendency to mistake undersized tankmates for food, it should be handled with care. *Habitat:* Tropical waters the world over. *Diet:* Chopped or whole shrimp and earthworms, depending on size, unwanted small fish.

PORKFISH (*Anistoremus virginicus*): Medium-sized and handsomely marked with orange and black stripes, this attractive marine fish, when young, is one of the few saltwater species displayed to advantage in schools and in relatively small aquaria. *Habitat:* Tropical western Atlantic Ocean. *Diet:* Varied, with chopped shrimp, earthworms, and small live fish.

PORT or **PORT ACARA:** see BLACK ACARA.

PORTUGUESE MAN-OF-WAR: any of several poisonous marine Siphonophores, or jellyfish (genus *Physalia*), a few species of which occasionally are introduced into home aquaria.

POWDER-BLUE SURGEONFISH (*Acanthurus leucosternon*): This uncommon but much sought after marine fish is largely a uniform light blue, with a black mask covering its face, a brilliant yellow dorsal fin edged in blue, a white anal fin, a yellow caudal peduncle, and a black-banded white tail. At some 8 inches in length, it is somewhat smaller than most surgeonfishes. *Habitat:* Widespread throughout Indo-Pacific waters. *Diet:* Most standard aquarium foods.

PRISTELLA: *see* X-RAY FISH.

PUFFER or **BLOWFISH:** any of numerous members of family TETRAODONTIDAE.

PUMPKINSEED: *see* SUNFISH.

PURPLE-STRIPED GUDGEON (*Mogurnda mogurnda*): This good-sized goby varies in color from one specimen to another, but usually is marked with black and red spots and with the three stripes on the cheek from which it takes its name. An incorrigible fin-nipper, it cannot be trusted in a community tank. *Habitat:* Australia. *Diet:* Live and frozen meaty foods.

PYGMY RASBORA: *see* SPOTTED RASBORA.

PYGMY SEA HORSE or **DWARF SEA HORSE** (*Hippocampus zosterae*): Related to the various pipefishes, this small, curious creature has an elongated tubelike snout, a covering of bony armor, and a prehensile tail. Sea horse eggs are carried by the male in a brood sac from which the minuscule but fully formed fry eventually issue forth. Pygmy sea horses are variable in coloration, hardy, inexpensive, quite easily bred, and enormously popular with both beginning and experienced saltwater aquarists. *Habitat:* Southern U.S. coastal waters. *Diet:* Live brine shrimp.

PYGMY SUNFISH (*Elassoma evergladei*): Not a true tropical fish, but native to the southern U.S., this small, lively creature is best kept with its own kind. An iridescent yellow-brown under favorable illumination, the male turns a rich gold-flecked black during the mating season. *Habitat:* The Carolinas south to Florida. *Diet:* Small live foods exclusively.

Q

QUARANTINE TANK: an aquarium maintained for the purpose of isolating newly obtained specimens from older fish until there is no danger of their transmitting infections, parasites, or the unnoticed larvae of predatory organisms. Proper maintanance of such tank requires that no equipment used in it be introduced into any other tanks.

QUEEN ANGELFISH: (*Angelichthys isabelita* or *Holocanthus ciliaris*): This large, stately yellow and blue fish from the coral reefs is immediately recognizable by the unusual spotted "crown" on its high forehead. One of the most popular of the marine fishes, it grows quite large and is unsuitable for small aquaria. *Habitat:* Tropical American Atlantic waters. *Diet:* Varied, with brine shrimp, chopped fresh shrimp, fish roe, and herbaceous matter preferred. NOTE: Baby brine shrimp should not be fed to larger specimens.

QUEEN TRIGGERFISH (*Balistes vetula*): A member of the family Balistidae, this large Atlantic marine fish, with its blue markings on a bright yellow ground, is extremely popular with home aquarists. Adult specimens are characterized by the attenuated tips of their caudal fins. *Habitat:* Coastal waters from Florida to Brazil. *Diet:* Live earthworms, minnows and small crabs, shrimp.

Queen Angelfish

R

RAINBOW FISH: An obsolete popular name for the GUPPY (*Lebistes reticulatus*).

RAINBOW TETRA (*Nematobrycon amphiloxus*): a small, shy golden-brown characin marked with blue spots above the dark lateral stripe that traverses the rear half of its body. *Habitat:* Colombia. *Diet:* Small live and frozen foods.

RAMIREZ' DWARF CICHLID or **RAM** (*Apistogramma ramirezi*): One of the smallest, handsomest, most popular and most peaceful of the cichlids, it is distinguished by its concave dorsal fin, subtly nuanced violet coloration, and a series of vertical bands, the most strongly defined of which runs through the eye. *Habitat:* Orinoco River basin. *Diet:* Small live foods.

RASBORA: any of some 45 species, all native to southeast Asia, of the genus *Rasbora* of family Cyprinidae. Typical examples are the HARLEQUIN FISH (*Rasbora heteromorpha*), the EXCLAMATION POINT RASBORA (*R. urophthalma*) and the BRILLIANT RASBORA (*R. einthoveni*).

RAY: any of numerous marine fishes of the order Rajiformes, having horizontally flattened bodies, a cartilaginous skeletal structure, and slender tails. Some young specimens are kept as curiosities by saltwater aquarists.

RED-BELLIED PIRANHA: see NATTERER'S PIRANHA.

Ramirez' Dwarf Cichlid or Ram

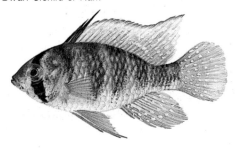

Red Discus or Pompadour

Redfin Butterflyfish

RED CICHLID: *see* JEWEL CICHLID.

RED DEVIL (*Cichlasoma erythraeum*): a large, ferocious, thick-lipped fish, often but not always red in color, sometimes with black mottlings on the fins, back, or lips. Altogether unsuited for life in community aquaria. *Habitat:* Central America. *Diet:* Small live or fresh filleted fish.

RED DISCUS or **POMPADOUR** (*Symphysoson discus*): At its best, this large, peaceful cichlid, its

wine-red, pancake-shaped body streaked with blue, rivals many marine fishes for sheer beauty and impressiveness of bearing. Parents of this species secrete a viscous body slime on which their newly hatched fry feed. *Habitat:* Amazon River region, Brazil. *Diet:* Varied live foods.

RED-EYED CHARACIN: *see* FIRE-MOUTH PANCHEX.

REDFIN BUTTERFLYFISH (*Chaetodon trifasciatus*): Splendidly marked in a curiously symmetrical fashion, this small, rather delicate yellow-orange marine fish looks much the same coming as going. Its boldest markings are vertical and located at the head and tial, with the central body markings much subtler. *Habitat:* Tropical Pacific waters from Hawaii to coastal Africa. *Diet:* Live foods, with live coral much preferred.

REDJAW KILLIE: *see* FIRE-MOUTH PANCHAX.

RED RAMSHORN (*Planorbis corneus*): the most popular of the various freshwater snails kept as scavengers by some aquarists.

RED-TAILED SHARK (*Labeo bicolor*): Jet black except for its red-orange caudal fin, this handsome, medium-sized cyprinid is peaceful toward other species, although the males can be quarrelsome among themselves. Given to browsing on algae. *Habitat:* Thailand. *Diet:* Varied live foods supplemented with herbaceous matter.

RED TETRA: *see* FLAME TETRA.

REGAL ANGELFISH (*Pygoplites diacanthus*): One of the most stunningly marked and colored of the Pacific marine fishes, this brilliant orange creature bears a series of somewhat crescent-shaped white bands, each boldly outlined in black, on its body, and an arresting striated pattern on its anal fin. Although well suited to community aquaria, it tends to outgrow all but the largest tanks. *Habitat:* Red Sea and tropical Pacific waters west of Hawaii. *Diet:* Varied, with paprika added for color tone.

Red-Tailed Shark

Regal Angelfish

REMORA: any of several long, slender marine fishes of the family Echeneidae, equipped with a sucking disk by which they cling to larger creatures. Occasionally collected by saltwater aquarists.

REPRODUCTION: Tropical fish engage in a variety of courtship, mating, and spawning rituals, some of them very simple and others quite elaborate. Superficial differences aside, however, the vast majority of species reproduce oviparously, which is to say, by the external hatching of eggs produced by the female and fertilized by the male. One taxonomic group (family Poecilidiidae), consisting of forty-odd known species and subspecies popularly termed "live-bearers," reproduces ovoviviparously. That is, the fertilized eggs are hatched internally within the female's brood pouch, after which the young issue forth from the mother's vent. To facilitate fertilization, nature provides the sexually mature male live-bearer with a gonopodium, a modification of the forerays of the anal fin, that is inserted into the female vent when fertilization is to take place. On superficial observation, the spawning process of the live-bearers may seem to be quite similar to the viviparous birth of mammals. The most apparent difference, however, is the absence of an umbilical cord, for at no time from conception to birth is the fetus actually connected to its mother. (Also *see* BREEDING TROPICAL FISH).

RIGHT: *Four characteristic spawning techniques.*

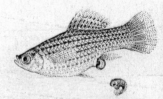

Female Guppy Delivering Her Young

Female Pelmatochromis laying her eggs

Male Betta stocking bubble nest with eggs

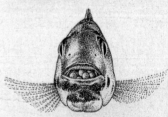

Male Tilapia with mouth full of incubating eggs

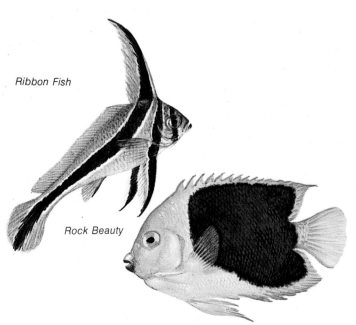

Ribbon Fish

Rock Beauty

RIBBON FISH or **JACKNIFE FISH** (*Equetus lanceolatus*): With its huge, maneuverable dorsal fin and striking markings, this black-banded creature is one of the most beautiful of the Atlantic marine fishes. Prone to travel in schools, it should not be kept with fin-nippers or other combative species. *Habitat:* Florida coastal and West Indian waters. *Diet:* Chopped shrimp, small live fish, brine shrimp and other small crustaceans.

RICE FISH: see MEDAKA.

RIO GRANDE PERCH or **TEXAS CICHLID** (*Herichthys cyanoguttatus*): The only cichlid found in U.S. waters, this large, bellicose fish has a blue-gray head and body that are liberally spangled with lighter blue or green spots. Although it is collected by some aquarists, it requires a large tank, is disruptive of plant and other fish life, and prefers a bare, unobstructed environment. On the other hand, it will survive much lower water temperatures than most cichlids. *Habitat:* South Texas and upper Mexico. *Diet:* Lean chunky meats, coarsely cut earthworms.

ROCK BEAUTY (*Holocanthus tricolor*): Orange and black with pale blue eyes, this shy marine angelfish is one of the most intensely colored of all sea creatures, When young, it bears a large, irregularly shaped, "soft-edged" black spot on the rear portion of its body. As the fish matures, the marking spreads to cover the fins and much more of the body. Extremely fragile in captivity, it is vulnerable to a number of

Royal Gramma

Rosy Tetra

diseases and, if exposed to too much light, blindness. *Habitat:* Outer reefs from Florida to the Bahamas. *Diet:* Brine shrimp, chopped fresh shrimp, algae, tubifex worms, with paprika added to heighten fish's color.

ROCK HIND (*Epinephelus adscensionis*): A large marine fish of the family Serranidae, this handsome red-spotted creature bears a dark oval marking, or "saddle," on its caudal peduncle. *Habitat:* Tropical Atlantic waters. *Diet:* Chopped shrimp, small live minnows, earthworms.

ROSY BARB (*Puntius conchonius*): This sizable, hardy, and very popular Asian minnow is most impressively colored during the mating period, when the normally silvery male takes on a rich claret

flush and the slightly larger female becomes more luminous. Both sexes bear a somewhat indistinct ocellus above the trailing edge of the anal fin. *Habitat:* India. *Diet:* All standard aquarium foods.

ROSY TETRA or **BLACK FLAG** (*Hyphessobrycon rosaceus*): At its best, swimming in a school under subdued light and against a dark ground, this peaceable little characin's body color constantly varies with changes in illumination or in the fish's own movement. Both the dorsal and anal fins of the male become gracefully attenuated with maturity and, in both sexes, the dorsal fin is largely black. *Habitat:* British Guiana and neighboring portions of Brazil. *Diet:* Varied, with small live and frozen foods preferred.

ROYAL GRAMMA (*Gramma loretto*): One of the smallest of the sea basses and one of the most highly colored, this charming creature makes its natural home in coral hollows. Suffused with a glowing violet tint over the forward two-thirds of its body length, its after end is a startling sulphur-yellow. A somewhat indolent swimmer, it will often hang motionless, its tail slanting downward. *Habitat:* Caribbean waters. *Diet:* Adult brine shrimp, unwanted fish fry, immature guppies and similar live foods.

RUBY TETRA (*Axelrodia riesei*): A diminutive, jewellike characin of a glowing red coloration, it adapts well to life with other small, peaceable species. *Habitat:* Colombia. *Diet:* Freeze-dried and very small live foods, with dry foods taken less enthusiastically.

SAILFIN MOLLY (*Mollienesia latipinna* or *Poecilia l.*): One of the most dramatic of the live-bearers, males of this perennially popular species are endowed with an inordinately large dorsal fin. Like the caudal fin, it takes on a heightened resplendency, shot through with blue and yellow iridescences, during its elaborate courtship ritual. Somewhat more difficult to breed than most gambusinos (and generally more difficult to maintain), gravid females should be disturbed as little as possible. *Habitat:* Coastal U.S. from North Carolina southward, the Florida Gulf Coast, northeastern Mexico. *Diet:* Algae (which should be cultivated in quantity) and other herbaceous matter of similar texture, cereals,

finely ground shrimp. NOTE: Requires high temperatures, well-aerated, slightly salt water, plenty of space, and frequent feedings.

SAILFIN TANG (*Zebrasoma veliferum*). Although otherwise similar in shape to most tangs, this sizable, variably colored, handsomely banded creature bears disproportionately large dorsal and anal fins. *Habitat:* Tropical Pacific waters from Hawaii to Africa. *Diet:* Dry foods, brine shrimp, tubifex, chopped shrimp, algae.

SALINITY: *see* WATER.

SALT WATER ITCH: *see* DISEASES OF TROPICAL FISH.

SAPROLEGNIA: *see* DISEASES OF TROPICAL FISH.

Sailfin Molly

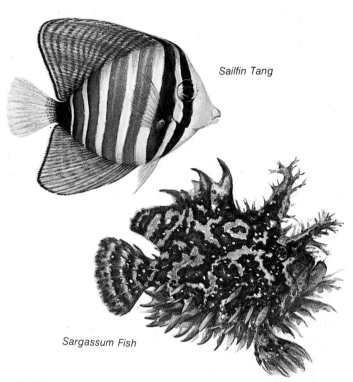

Sailfin Tang

Sargassum Fish

SARAPO: *see* BANDED KNIFE FISH.

SARGASSUM FISH (*Histrio histrio*): Camouflaged to look like a piece of the floating seaweed amidst which it lives, this curious little creature is a voracious predator that will swallow anything it encounters, including members of its own species almost as large as itself. Easily maintained in saltwater aquaria, it should, of course, be isolated from smaller fish. *Habitat:* Tropical seas throughout the world. *Diet:* Live fish and earthworms, fresh shrimp.

SCALARE: *see* ANGELFISH.

SCALLOP: any of numerous free-swimming marine mollusks of the family Pectinidae, having fluted, fan-shaped bivalve shells, of which a few, such as the flame scallop (*Lima scabra*), are introduced into saltwater aquaria as novelties.

SCARF-TAIL GUPPY: a fancy variety, selectively bred, of the common guppy (*Lebistes reticulatus*), distinguished by the scarf-like appearance of its oversized caudal fin.

SCARIDAE: the taxonomic family comprising the PARROT FISH.

155

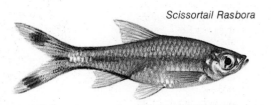

Scissortail Rasbora

SCAT: any of numerous large, vertically flattened Asian estuarial fishes, such as the spotted scat (*Scatophagus argus*), related to the marine angelfishes and displayed in both marine and freshwater aquaria.

SCATOPHAGIDAE: the taxonomic family made up of various fishes commonly known at SCATS.

SCAVENGER: any of various fishes, such as many catfishes, snails, and other aquatic organisms that live wholly or in part by rooting or foraging for food uneaten by other fishes, accumulated algae, dead fishes, and the like. Many aquarists introduce scavengers of one sort or another into community tanks as aids to sanitation.

SCISSORTAIL RASBORA (*Rasbora trilineata*): This large, silvery, semitranslucent minnow, like several other fishes, activates its forward motion by rapidly opening and closing the two lobes of its caudal fin in a scissorlike fashion. Each of these lobes, in the case of *R. trilineata*, is emphatically marked with a sloping black bar that together imply a backward-pointing letter **V**. The fish also is marked with three somewhat indistinct horizontal stripes. Extremely

mobile, peaceful, hardy, and easily bred, it is a very popular species despite its rather nondescript appearance. *Habitat:* Malaysia. *Diet:* Omnivorous

SCORPAENIDAE: the taxonomic family embracing the marine scorpion fishes of the order Cataphracti, which are characterized by the enlargement of one of the cheekbones and whose spines often are venomous. The best-known of the scorpion fishes is the LIONFISH.

SEA ANEMONE: *see* ANEMONE.

SEA HORSE (*Hippocampus*): any of several small marine fishes of the family Syngnathidae, related to the pipefishes and, like them, characterized by an elongated tubular snout and a bony outer covering. Unlike other fishes, the sea horses swim in an upright or vertical position and are equipped with prehensile tails. Found in many parts of the world, various sea horses, such as *H. hudsonius* of the American Atlantic Coast, are kept by marine aquarists. They are prized for such interesting features as their equine appearance, their ability to swim or "hover" without apparent means of locomotion (actually, they propel themselves by fluttering their transparent, nearly invisible dorsal fins), and the brood sac in which the male carries the young until they are fully formed. Sea horses are not difficult to raise and make exceptionally agreeable pets but, with rare exceptions, will eat only live foods. (Also *see* PYGMY SEA HORSE.)

SEA LICE: *see* DISEASES OF TROPICAL FISH.

SERGEANT MAJOR (*Abudefduf saxitilis*): Perhaps the commonest of the saltwater aquarium fishes, this fast-swimming little yellow-and-black creature normally bears five vertical bars on its body, but its coloration and markings tend to vary with the condition of its health and the intensity of the illumination to which it is exposed. *Habitat:* Tropical waters on both coasts of the Americas. *Diet:* Varied.

SERPA TETRA: *see* CALLISTUS TETRA.

SERRANIDAE: the taxonomic family comprising the marine groupers and sea basses, many of which are common food fish. All serranid fishes are protandric hermaphrodites, *i.e.*, male at birth, but capable of changing sex as they mature.

Sea Horse

Sergeant Major

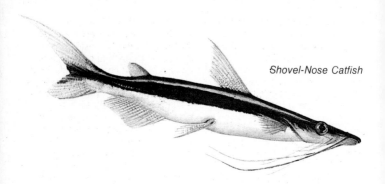
Shovel-Nose Catfish

SHIMMIES: *see* DISEASES OF TROPICAL FISH.

SHOCK: *see* DISEASES OF TROPICAL FISH.

SHOVEL-NOSE CATFISH (*Sorubim lima*):This large, curious, nocturnal pimelodid catfish is endowed with an elongated snout and barbels and a large adipose fin. Generally olive or gray, it is marked with darker horizontal stripes on the back and sides. It can be kept in large community tanks, but is inclined to prey on unwary small fishes in confined spaces. *Habitat:* Uruguay, eastern Argentina. *Diet:* Omnivorous.

SHOWING TROPICAL FISH: While the practice of holding competitive exhibitions is not nearly as widespread among tropical fish enthusiasts as it is among dog, cat, horse, and bird lovers, livestock breeders, gardeners, and other hobbyists, both interclub and open shows are proliferating at a pace more or less commensurate with the general increase of interest in the tropical fish hobby itself. By and large, such shows conform to the general format of most pet exhibitions, with competitions held for various categories of fishes and, less frequently, with several prizes awarded for outstanding specimens regardless of type. As is not the case with most animal shows, however, a mated pair, and not a single specimen, usually constitutes an entry, with any two fish of the same species, mated or not, permissible in cases where no external sexual characteristics exist. In most competitions, judgements are based on three criteria: Condition and style; quality of color; and relative size. Most scoring systems award a maximum of 40, 40, and 20 points respectively in these categories. Exceptions to this general rule apply to various species or hybrids prized for certain specific characteristics. Certain types of fish cultivated for their disproportionately large fins, for example, might be judged on the relative size and shape of such attributes and not on the size of the fish as a whole.

In addition to the foregoing, many tropical-fish shows feature an aquarium competition based on such considerations as: Condition, variety, and rarity of the fish displayed; design of the aquarium itself; arrangement, condition, and rarity of aquatic plants displayed; general artistic effect; and condition and suitability of other fauna housed in the tank. In the more important open shows, entrants are expected to display aquaria within the exhibition area. In smaller local shows, however, the usual practice is for a committee of visiting judges to inspect aquaria in the homes of the competitors. Competition in both open and interclub shows usually is restricted to amateurs, although professional exhibits and separate professional competitions increasingly are included in the larger open shows.

As yet, there is no generalized governing body, either international or national, empowered to standardize exhibiton scoring systems. As the number of tropical fish enthusiasts throughout the world increases, however, it is only a question of time before such bodies are organized.

This tank of ornate goldfish is just waiting for a winner's ribbon to be fixed to the tank side.

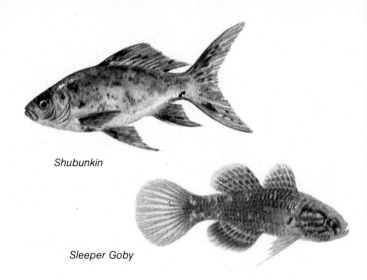

Shubunkin

Sleeper Goby

SHUBUNKIN: a variegated form of the goldfish (*Carassius auratus*), usually marked with irregular red, yellow, black, and white streaks on a deep blue ground.

SIAMESE FIGHTING FISH: *see* BETTA.

SICKLE BARB (*Puntius wohlerti*): A small slender, shy, and somewhat obscure yellow-brown fish marked with a violet horizontal stripe, it takes its name from the male's sickle-shaped anal fin. *Habitat:* East Africa. *Diet:* Small live and frozen foods.

SILURIDAE: the taxonomic family comprised of the silurid catfishes of the Old World, characterized by the disproportionate length of the anal fin and a merely vestigial or altogether absent dorsal fin.

SILVER DOLLAR: the popular name given to a number of flat, silvery characins of various species or genera.

SILVER-TIP TETRA (*Hemigrammus nanus*): This small, peaceful brown characin, distinguished by the silvery tips on its fins, is best displayed in schools and against a dark background. *Habitat:* Southeastern Brazil. *Diet:* Varied smaller foods.

SIMPSON SWORDTAIL or **SIMPSON HI-FIN SWORD:** a mutant variety of the common swordtail or helleri (*Xiphophorus helleri*), selectively bred to produce a tall, trailing dorsal fin.

SIX-BANDED BARB (*Barbus hexazona*): This medium-sized, otherwise typical yellow-brown barb bears six dark vertical bars, one of which runs through the eye. Peaceable and well-behaved in community tanks, the adult male is distinguished by the red flush that suffuses the bases of its fins. *Habitat:* Malay Peninsula. *Diet:* Varied small foods.

SLEEPER GOBY or **SPOTTED SLEEPER** (*Dormitator maculatus*): This large, somewhat torpid but voracious, irregularly marked greenish-brown fish is found in salt, brackish, and fresh American coastal waters. Flecked with blue behind the gill plate, its eye also gleams blue in certain lights. Should not be kept with smaller fishes. *Habitat:* The western Atlantic Coast from the Carolinas southward to Brazil. *Diet:* Omnivorous.

SLIPPERY DICK (*Halichores bivittatus*): Largely because of its prevalence throughout western Atlantic and Caribbean waters, this is one of the fishes most commonly encountered in American home aquaria. Medium sized and quite adaptable to life in captivity, it is a long, slender yellow-pink creature with a broad lateral stripe extending from the snout to the caudal fin.

Habitat: Reefs from the southern U.S. to Brazil. *Diet:* Marine invertebrates and most meaty aquarium foods.

SNAIL: any of innumerable gastropod mollusks, characteristically housed in a spiral-shaped shell and having a broad retractable foot, distinct head, and retractile eye-stalks. Of the numerous aquatic snails, several freshwater and marine species are kept by home aquarists, usually as aids to keeping tanks free of algae.

SNAKEHEADS: *see* CHANNIDAE.

SNAKESKIN GOURAMI (*Trichogaster pectoralis*): A particularly desirable addition to community tanks stocked with larger fish, this attractive bubble-nest builder is hardy, peaceable, easily bred, and takes all foods enthusiastically. Marked with a series of close-spaced yellow diagonal bars on a darker olive-green or gray-green

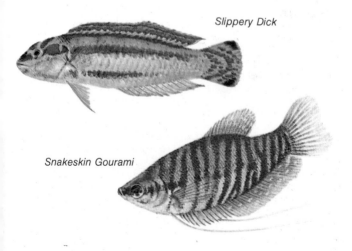

Slippery Dick

Snakeskin Gourami

ground, it also has a broken horizontal stripe running the length of the body, and a pair of filamentlike ventral fins. *Habitat:* Malay Peninsula. *Diet:* Omnivorous.

SOLE or **BROAD-SOLE:** any of numerous flatfishes of the family Achiridae, all of which lie on one side, have both eyes on the opposite, or topmost, side, and are further characterized by their twisted mouths. Small or immature soles of various species are kept as curiosities by both freshwater and marine aquarists.

SOUTH AMERICAN PUFFER (*Colomesus psittacus*): Of the various freshwater blowfishes, this small, handsome, irregularly banded creature is one of the best-suited to life in community aquaria, at least so long as it is kept with fish it cannot swallow. Olive or brown above and white-bellied, it swims with the hovering motion common to most puffers. *Habitat:* Northern Brazil, the Guianas,

Venezuela. *Diet:* Larger live foods, small crustaceans and snails, unwanted small fish.

SPANNER BARB or **T-BARB** (*Barbodes lateristriga*): a sizable and unusually marked minnow bearing two vertical bands on the forward half of its yellow-green body and a horizontal stripe from the middle of the body to the base of the tail. These markings grow less distinct as the fish matures. *Habitat:* Malay Peninsula and its environs. *Diet:* Omniverous, with live foods preferred.

SPHENOPS or **MOLLY** (*Mollie-nesia sphenops* or *Poecilia mexicana*): One of the most popular and best-known of all freshwater aquarium fishes, this small live-bearer is less fragile than most mollies and less fussy about its diet and environment. Variously colored and marked, it is most commonly all-black, mottled black, or greenish-gray, with the male's caudal fin often edged in orange.

South American Puffer

Spanner Barb

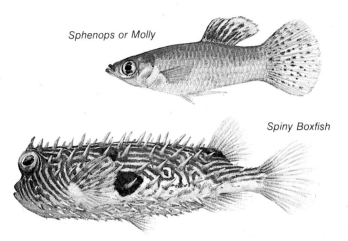

Sphenops or Molly

Spiny Boxfish

Habitat: Mexico southward to upper South America. *Diet:* Brine shrimp and similar foods, herbaceous matter.

SPINED LOACH: *see* SPOTTED WEATHERFISH.

SPINY BOXFISH (*Chilomycterus schoepfii*): This hardy, active marine blowfish bears mazelike markings that resemble elaborate doodles and is covered with a bristling array of spikelike defensive protuberances, of which those on the belly are erectile. Easily tamed and extremely variable in size, it is most popular with aquarists when less than an inch long. Like most blowfish, it is equipped with powerful jaws capable of inflicting painful bites. *Habitat:* Coastal waters from New England to Florida. *Diet:* (larger adults) Chopped shrimp and small live fish, earthworms; (smaller specimens) live brine shrimp, tubifex worms, finely ground fresh shrimp.

SPINY CATFISH or **TALKING CATFISH** (*Acanthodoras spinosissimus*): This sizable nocturnal creature, somewhat shy and fond of burying itself in gravel, emits a faint croaking sound, hence the popular name "talking catfish." Light brown with darker mottlings, it requires dark hiding places and should be handled with care. *Habitat:* Central Amazon region. *Diet:* Small live foods.

SPINY EEL: any of several eel-like members of the family Mastocembelidae, of which *Mastacembelus maculatus* and *M. armatus* are among the best known. Adults of the former species are handsome, but difficult to handle and far too large for most home aquaria. The latter, smaller but also hard to handle, habitually buries itself in gravel tank beds, resting there with only its eyes and snout protruding. Native to India and Southeast Asia, the spiny eels are largely nocturnal.

Spotted Danio

Spotted Leporinus

SPLASH TETRA: *see* JUMPING CHARACIN.

SPLIT-TAILED BETTA: a mutant version of the betta or Siamese fighting fish (*Betta splendens*), its most distinctive characteristic is its bifurcated caudal fin.

SPOTTED BARB (*Barbodes binotatus*): a large, active, rather drab fish, its minimal popularity is in no way enhanced by its pugnacity, insatiable appetite, and tendency to uproot decorative plants. *Habitat:* Southeast Asia. *Diet:* Omnivorous.

SPOTTED DANIO (*Brachydanio nigrofasciatus*): Hardy, active, and peaceful, this attractive little minnow is best displayed in schools. Its brown back is divided from its yellowish belly by a handsome stripe that begins behind the gill and comes to a tapering point at the end of the caudal fin. A series of spots runs beneath this stripe for much of its length. *Habitat:* Burma. *Diet:* Varied small foods.

SPOTTED HEADSTANDER (*Chilodus punctatus*): This peaceful characin is relatively colorless, but its handsomely patterned scales catch and reflect light like so many faceted gems. Given to hovering in an oblique position with its head downward, it makes an interesting, if somewhat aloof, addition to the community aquarium. *Habitat:* The Guianas and their environs. *Diet:* Largely herbaceous; leafy green vegetables should be supplemented with dry and live foods.

SPOTTED LEPORINUS (*Leporinus maculatus*): Its tan body covered with large black spots, this striking characin is peaceful and easily kept, but requires a covered tank. *Habitat:* Widespread throughout South America from the Guianas to São Paulo. *Diet:* Varied, with herbaceous matter eagerly accepted.

SPOTTED RASBORA or **PYGMY RASBORA** (*Rasbora maculata*): A diminutive red-orange carp bearing a round black spot on its side, this peaceful creature is shown to best advantage in full natural sunlight against a dark ground. *Habitat:* India, Malay Peninsula, Sunda Islands. *Diet:* Varied small foods. NOTE: Acid, very soft water required.

SPOTTED SCAT (*Scatophagus argus*): Large, hardy, and impressive, this usually silver-brown creature is indigenous to estuarial waters and can be kept in both freshwater and marine aquaria. Shaped rather like a blunt arrowhead when seen in silhouette, the fish's body is horizontally flattened, with its rounded forward outline barely broken by the receding head. Peaceful with other species, but destructive of plants. *Habitat:* Coastal, brackish, and sometimes upstream East Indian waters. *Diet:* Various live foods generously supplemented with herbaceous matter.

SPOTTED SLEEPER: *see* SLEEPER GOBY.

SPOTTED WEATHERFISH or **SPINED LOACH** (*Cobitis taenia*): Like several other members of family Cobitidae, this handsomely marked yellow-brown loach is reputed to be something of a meteorologist, legend having it that the fish's activity heightens or lessens with increases and decreases of barometric pressure. Elongated and rather shy, it bears a movable spine below each eye and has six barbels on the upper jaw. *Habitat:* Widespread in various regions of Europe and Asia. *Diet:* Omnivorous, with small live worms preferred.

SPRAYING CHARACIN: *see* JUMPING CHARACIN.

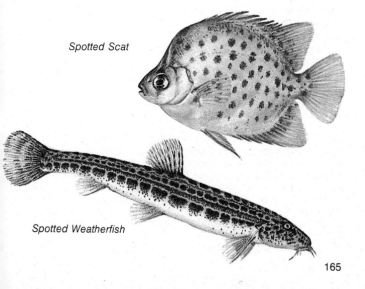

Spotted Scat

Spotted Weatherfish

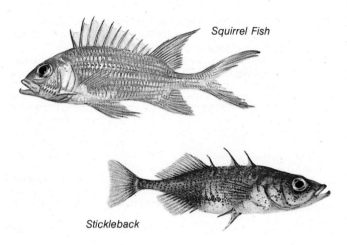

Squirrel Fish

Stickleback

SQUIRRELFISH: (1) Any of various marine fishes belonging to the family Holocentridae and usually red or reddish in color, with an emphatically notched dorsal fin and scissor tail; (2) specifically *Adioryx diadema* (also called barred squirrelfish), a largely nocturnal, big-eyed, vividly striped, very popular aquarium fish. *Habitat:* Hawaiian Islands, western Pacific, Red Sea. *Diet:* Chopped fish and shrimp, unwanted small aquarium fish.

STARFISH: any of numerous invertebrate marine echinoderms of the class Asteroidea, most commonly of a radially symmetrical shape with five tapering tentacles, equipped with suction discs, extending from a central hub. Various common starfishes (*e.g. Hippasteria spinosa*) are kept as curiosities in home aquaria, where they usually thrive on chopped shrimp and small shellfish.

STICKLEBACK: any of several species of the family Gasterosteidae, native to coastal and brackish waters of the Northern Hemisphere. They characteristically bear a number of free-standing spines forward of the dorsal fin and are given to an elaborate courtship ritual involving considerable engineering of tunnels and nests. Although not true tropical fish, such sticklebacks as *Apeltes quadracus* and *Gasterosteus aculeatus* are kept by some home aquarists, but should never be introduced into community tanks. Both the aforementioned species are native to North America, and all sticklebacks should be fed small live foods exclusively.

STRIPED BARB (*Barbodes fasciatus* or *Barbus f.*): Like most barbs, this horizontally-striped silvery-yellow species is quite active and gets along well with other fishes. *Habitat:* Malay Peninsula, Sunda Islands. *Diet:* Most standard aquarium foods.

STRIPED GOURAMI: *see* GIANT GOURAMI.

STRIPED HEADSTANDER (*Anostomus anostomus*): A large, handsome, long-bodied characin, vividly marked with two golden horizontal stripes that run the full length of its dark-brown sides, this is a peaceful fish whose most distinctive characteristic is its upturned mouth. *Habitat:* The Guianas and, less commonly, the Amazon region. *Diet:* Varied, with live and herbaceous foods preferred.

STRIPED LEPORINUS (*Leporinus striatus*): an extremely active, good-sized strongly marked fish bearing alternating black and yellow stripes that run horizontally from the snout to the caudal base. Like many other characins, it is an incurable jumper and must be kept in a covered tank. *Habitat:* Central South America. *Diet:* Omnivorous, with frequent supplements of herbaceous matter.

SUCKER CATFISH (*Hypostomus plecostomus*): Resembling a throwback to some early form of earthly life, this large, useful scavenger's sole claim to physical beauty is its large, crestlike, spotted dorsal fin. Largely nocturnal, mottled to resemble stream bottoms, and equipped with a vacuum cleanerlike mouth, it behaves well in community tanks. *Habitat:* Upper South America and the West Indies. *Diet:* Live, fresh, or frozen meaty foods, algae.

SUMATRA BARB: *see* TIGER BARB.

SUNFISH or **PUMPKINSEED** (*Lepomis gibbosus*): Not a true tropical fish and unsuited for fraternization with true tropicals, this sizable, iridescent creature is

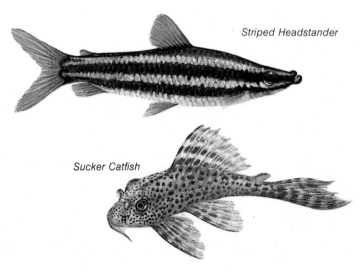

Striped Headstander

Sucker Catfish

Sunset Hi-Fin Variatus

Swordtail

nonetheless prized by some aquarists, particularly in Europe. *Habitat:* The eastern half of the U.S. *Diet:* Large live and coarse meaty foods. NOTE: Thrives in water too cold for true tropicals.

SUNSET GOURAMI: *see* HONEY GOURAMI.

SUNSET HI-FIN VARIATUS: a red-bodied hybrid PLATY characterized by its oversized yellow dorsal fin.

SUNSET PLATY: a hybrid PLATY, usually with yellow-to-green body color (in the male), yellow dorsal, and red caudal fins.

SURGEON FISH: any of several related marine fishes, such as the Pacific yellow tang (*Zebrasoma flavescens*) or Atlantic yellow tang (*Acanthurus unicolor*) known for their vivid color.

SWAMP BARB (*Capoeta chola*): Silver-bodied with a greenish shimmer, this fair-sized carp bears a black spot near the base of its tail and a less distinct red spot on the gill cover. Peaceful and active. *Habitat:* India, Burma. *Diet:* Most standard aquarium foods.

SWIM BLADDER DISEASE *see* DISEASES OF TROPICAL FISH.

SWORDTAIL or **SWORD** or **HELLERI** (*Xiphophorus helleri*): an extremely popular live-bearer which, by selective breeding, has produced many color varieties. The green swordtail, the original strain, is distinguished by the male's surprisingly attenuated "sword," a curious appendage of the lower lobe of the caudal fin that usually is somewhat shorter in highly bred strains. Readily mated and quite attractive, swordtails are among the largest and most active of the gambusinos and require ample space in covered tanks. Fancy varieties of the species include the red-eyed, red wagtail, and berlin swordtails. *Habitat:* Mexico and Central America. *Diet:* All standard aquarium foods, algae.

SWORDTAIL CHARACIN (*Corynopoma riisei*): Males of this rather mysterious species are characterized by attenuated finnage and curious filamentlike extensions of the gill plates—extensions that culminate in discs that extend at right angles from the body during the courtship display. Observers have yet to determine when or how fertilization of the female's eggs occurs, with various theories of greater or lesser plausibility having been advanced. The fish is silvery, with a dark horizontal stripe running from behind the gill cover to the end of the caudal fin. The male, although fairly small, is larger than the female. *Habitat:* Northwestern South America, Trinidad. *Diet:* Varied, with small live foods preferred.

SYNGNATHIDAE: the saltwater taxonomic family made up of the various SEA HORSES and PIPEFISHES.

Swordtail Characin

T

TAIL ROT: *see* DISEASES OF TROPICAL FISH.

TALKING CATFISH: *see* SPINY CATFISH.

TARGET FISH: *see* JARBUA.

T-BARB: *see* SPANNER BARB.

TELESCOPE FANTAIL GOLD-FISH: a selectively bred fancy variety of the common goldfish (*Carassius auratus*) characterized by a graceful veillike tail and protuberant eyes.

TEMPERATURE, WATER: *see* WATER.

TETRA: originally, a popular diminutive for the genus *Tetragonopterus* of the family Characidae, the term loosely applied to such characins as the neon, lemon, black, and silver tetras.

TET (RA) FROM RIO: *see* FLAME TETRA.

TETRAODONTIDAE: the taxonomic family embracing the marine PUFFERS or blowfishes, which characteristically inflate their bodies with water or air when in danger, and which are further typified by the parrotlike beak formed by the fusion of their teeth. (Also *see* COMMON PUFFER-FISH.)

TETRA PEREZ: *see* BLEEDING HEART TETRA.

TETRA SERPAE (*Hyphessobrycon serpae*): Although itself diminutive, this red-tailed, olive-backed, silver-bellied characin tends to bully and nip the fins of smaller species. *Habitat:* Amazon River region. *Diet:* Varied aquarium foods. NOTE: Subject to considerable nomenclatural confusion, with both the popular and scientific names disputed or assigned to other species.

False Ulreyi

TEXAS CICHLID: *see* RIO GRANDE PERCH.

THAYER'S CICHLID: *see* FLAG CICHLID.

THERAPONIDAE: the taxonomic designation for the various tiger-fishes, which are native to fresh, salt, or brackish water, and of which one of the best known is the JARBUA (*Therapon jarbua*).

THERMOSTAT: an electrically-operated device, submersible or externally attached, employed to control the WATER temperature in tropical fish aquaria.

THICK-LIPPED GOURAMI (*Colisa labiosa*): A medium-sized, blue-bodied anabantid, indistinctly marked with several dark vertical bands and, frequently, a blue horizontal stripe. Well-behaved in community aquaria, but vulnerable to fin-nipping species. *Habitat:*

India, Burma. *Diet:* Varied, with live foods preferred.

THREE-SPOT GOURAMI (*Trichogaster trichopterus*): this large, easily bred bubble-nest builder is marked with two distinct spots, one amidships and one at the caudal base, and a less clearly defined spot behind the gill cover. Its habits are similar to those of such other anabantids as the thick-lipped gourami (above). *Habitat:* Malay Peninsula and its environs. *Diet:* Varied, with live foods preferred.

TIC-TAC-TOE BARB: *see* TWO-SPOT BARB.

TIGER BARB or **SUMATRA BARB** (*Capoeta tetrazona*): Very popular and readily available, this active, fast-swimming barb is inclined to nip the fins of its more stately tankmates, but this propensity is less pronounced when it is

Thick-Lipped Gourami

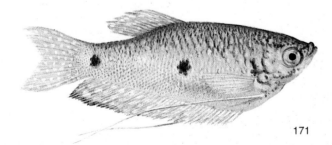

171

Topsail Variatus

provided with the company of its own kind. Yellow-bodied with four distinct black vertical bands, one running through the eye, it has dorsal, ventral, and caudal fins striped or tinged with red. *Habitat:* Sunda Islands. *Diet:* Varied small foods supplemented with algae or other herbaceous matter.

TIGER BOTIA: *see* CLOWN LOACH.

TINFOIL BARB (*Barbodes schwanenfeldi*): Although a peaceful, attractive fish with red-orange fins and a silvery body, it has the drawbacks that go with great size and a healthy appetite for decorative plants. *Habitat:* Thailand, Malay Archipelago. *Diet:* Varied, with herbaceous matter eagerly accepted.

TOPSAIL VARIATUS: a selectively bred fancy platy prized for its disproportionately large, flowing yellow dorsal fin. Although body color varies from one specimen to another, the caudal fin usually is red.

TOWNSEND ANGELFISH (*Angelichthys townsendi*): Perhaps the most colorful of the Atlantic Ocean angelfishes, this large, imposing creature is distinctively marked with broad bands of deep blue and vivid orange. Unfortunately, it tends to grow somewhat pale in captivity, but even faded specimens are among the most stunning of aquarium fish. *Habitat:* Offshore waters of Florida and the Bahamas. *Diet:* (small specimens) Live brine shrimp and comparable small foods; (larger specimens) coarsely chopped fresh shrimp, earthworms, lean meaty foods, frequently supplemented with paprika.

TRANSLUCENT BLOODFIN or **GLASS BLOODFIN** (*Priono-brama filigera*): *Very similar to, and often mistaken for, the* BLOODFIN (*Aphyocharax rubripinnis*), this small characin is distinguished by the sickle-shaped, white-edged anal fin of the male. *Habitat:* Amazon basin. *Diet:* Varied, with small live foods preferred.

TRAUMATIC DISEASES: *see* DISEASES OF TROPICAL FISH.

TRIGGER FISH: *see* BALISTIDAE.

TRUNKFISH: *see* OSTRACIIDAE.

TUBERCULOSIS: *see* DISEASES OF TROPICAL FISH.

TUBIFEX: a small, slender red aquatic worm, commonly found in colonies at the bottoms of ponds or other bodies of water rich in organic wastes. One of the commonest and most nutritious of the small live aquarium foods, tubifex are procurable at many aquarium supply shops in live or freeze-dried form. Freshly caught tubifex should not be introduced directly into aquaria, which they may infect with various waste-borne diseases, but should first be allowed to cleanse themselves thoroughly in running water.

TURKEYFISH: *see* LIONFISH.

TWO-SPOT BARB or **TIC-TAC-TOE BARB** (*Puntius ticto*): Although far from being the most colorful of the barbs, this fair-sized creature is prized for its iridescence and the red edging on its dorsal fin, which takes on a deep ruby hue during mating periods. Well-behaved in community tanks, except for larger specimens, which are inclined to be pugnacious, it bears two irregular spots on each side of the body. *Habitat:* Sri Lanka. *Diet:* Standard aquarium foods, with live foods preferred.

U

UMBRELLA DWARF CICHLID (*Apistogramma borelli*): This small yellow-gray creature is of greatest interest during the courtship and spawning ritual, when the usually nondescript male becomes suffused with color in response to the elaborate enticements of the female, who then banishes her mate as soon as her bright red eggs have been fertilized. *Habitat:* Widespread throughout the southern half of South America. *Diet:* Varied; small live foods preferred.

UNDULATE TRIGGERFISH or **ORANGE-STRIPED TRIGGERFISH** (*Balistapus undulatus*).

Undulate Triggerfish

Upside-Down Catfish

Although aggressive, voracious, and generally disruptive, this medium-sized marine triggerfish is much prized for its arresting orange patterns (striations over much of the body, a "saddle" of dots on its snout), and an elongated outline that makes its relatively small mouth appear to extend almost back to its anal fin. *Habitat:* Widespread throughout the Pacific Ocean and Red Sea. *Diet:* Omnivorous.

UPSIDE-DOWN CATFISH (*Synodontis nigriventris*): Large-eyed and given to swimming in a variety of unconventional positions, this mochokid catfish makes an amusing addition to community aquaria. Marked with gray and black mottlings on a yellow-to-olive ground, it bears branched barbels on the lower lip. *Habitat:* Congo River basin and its environs. *Diet:* All standard aquarium foods, scavenged material.

URUGUAY CHARACIN (*Pedalibrycon felipponei*): Disruptive in community aquaria and nondescript in appearance, this silver-gray fish is not much sought after by hobbyists. It has an underslung jaw and bears a black spot on the caudal fin. *Habitat:* Uruguay. *Diet:* Omnivorous.

V

VARIEGATED PLATY (*Xiphophorus variatus*): The product of hybridization and cross breeding, the variegated platy takes a number of fancy forms, with males usually bearing irregular markings and color patterns, while the females tend toward single solid colors. *Habitat:* Man-controlled environments. *Diet:* All standard aquarium foods.

VEIL ANGELFISH: a fancy variety of the common ANGELFISH (*Pterophyllum scalare*), selectively bred to produce flowing, beil-like finnage.

VEILTAIL GUPPY: an aquarium-bred fancy variety of the common GUPPY (*Lebistes reticulatus*), prized for its rainbowlike color and elongated flowing tail.

VELVET: *see* DISEASES OF TROPœICAL FISH.

Veiltail guppy

Variegated Platy

176

WAGTAIL PLATY: an aquarium-bred strain of the common PLATY (*Xiphophorus maculatus*), recognizable by its red or golden body and black fins.

WATER: This, of course, is the element in which, with very few exceptions, all fish spend their entire lives. Obviously then, its condition and quality are the overriding determinant in the success or failure of the aquarium. Without healthful water, no aquarium can maintain healthy fish. Naturally, any water introduced into an aquarium should be properly aerated and filtered, free of all potentially dangerous organisms, irritants, and injurious chemicals, and maintained at recommended temperatures.

In its pure state, water is a limpid, odorless, tasteless liquid, colorless in small or thinly spread quantities, but blue-tinged when seen in bulk, and made up of two parts hydrogen to one part oxygen, a formula expressed by the familiar symbol H_2O. Pure water is usually obtainable only at some expense, however, and for all practical purposes the water we use contains a variety of chemicals and trace elements. Many of these chemicals can be beneficial, injurious, or benign, depending on their degree of incidence and on the requirements of the organisms exposed to them. In the case of tropical fish and aquatic plants, some species require a high calcium content, which, with magnesium salts, is found in what usually is termed "hard" water; others have little tolerance for these chemicals and thrive best in "soft" water. Similarly, some fish are best served by a highly acid environment, or water rich in hydrogen ions, while others thrive on alkalinity.

Limestone is one of the commonest sources of calcium carbonate ($CaCO_3$) in water, and its presence in quantity usually makes itself known when soaps fail to produce lather. Aquarists are understandably reluctant to use this test in its most direct form, which is imprecise at best, and for the most part employ either of two commercially available testing devices. One of them actually involves the use of soap (but not in the aquarium), while the other employs solutions that produce color changes. At least three measurement scales are employed to express the relative hardness of water: ppm, or parts per millions of $CaCO_3$ to water; Dh, or parts per

pH COLOR COMPARISON CHART

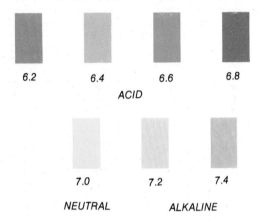

6.2   6.4   6.6   6.8

ACID

7.0   7.2   7.4

NEUTRAL   *ALKALINE*

100,000 of $CaCO_3$ to water; and Clark degres, or the number of grains of $CaCO_3$ per gallon of water. Soft water contains from 0 to 3.5 Clark degrees, while hard water ranges from 10.5° to 21°, with 1° equal to 14 ppm or $^4/_5$ Dh.

The relative acidity or alkalinity of water, expressed by its pH value, is measured according to a 0-to-14 scale—neutral water registering 7, with all numbers below 7 in the acid range, and with all numbers above 7 indicating ascending degrees of alkalinity. Several types of test kits employ color dyes to measure pH value and are available at most commercial aquarium supply sources. Information concerning the tolerances of given species for relative hardness, pH values, and temperatures should be sought at the source of supply.

For marine aquarists, the major consideration concerning water, temperature aside, has to do with its specific gravity—in effect, its degree of salinity—which is measured with an inexpensive hydrometer available at all marine aquarium supply houses. Most saltwater fishes have a reasonably broad adaptive range, but those native to coral reef waters thrive best at a reading of 1.025, the equivalent of a 3.5% salt content.

WAVY CATFISH (*Corydoras undulatus* or *C. microps*): This average-sized *Corydoras* differs from its near-relatives chiefly in its undulating pattern of black dots on a yellow-to-olive ground and its disinclination to scavenge. *Habitat:* Eastern South America. *Diet:* Small live foods.

WHIPTAIL(ED) CATFISH or **WHIPTAIL LORICARIA** (*Loricaria parva*): Camouflaged to blend with stream bottoms, this armored suckermouth is one of the most effective of the algae scavengers. The upper lobe of the caudal fin, at the end of a long, tapering body, bears a threadlike attenuation or "whip." *Habitat:* Central South America. *Diet:* Small live foods that settle on the bottom (*e.g.* tubifex worms) and herbaceous matter.

WHITE CLOUD MOUNTAIN MINNOW: the common name for either of two similar but distinct fishes found in the streams of the White Cloud Mountain in south-eastern China, *Tanichthys albonubes* and *Aphyocypris pooni*, of which the latter's fins are more distinctly yellow-edged. Small, hardy, peaceful, easily bred, and extremely attractive, they are among the most suitable species for the neophyte aquarist. Displayed to best advantage in schools, they have green backs, red-spotted tails, and when young a luminescent blue-green stripe running from behind the eye to the caudal base (this stripe gradually dulls as the fish matures). They are not true tropical fish and should not be mixed with species requiring water temperatures of more than 70°F. *Habitat:* Vicinity of Canton, China. *Diet:* Varied smaller foods, with frequent feedings recommended. NOTE: Both species are known by several close variants of the popular name given here.

WHITE PATCH: *see* DISEASES OF TROPICAL FISH.

WHITE PIRANHA or **SPOTTED PIRANHA** (*Serrasalmus rhombeus*): While many of the various piranhas are less ferocious than they are reputed to be, this one is the notorious "Terror of the Amazon," whose wolflike propensities, usually much exaggerated, have become the stuff of legend. In captivity, single piranhas hardly live up

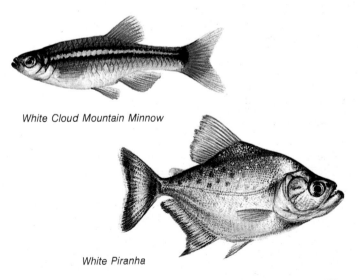

White Cloud Mountain Minnow

White Piranha

to their reputation and in fact behave rather shyly. Nonetheless, the white piranha, a silver-white fish with a spangling of small gray spots, is a large creature with razor-sharp teeth and traplike jaws, and should be handled accordingly. *Habitat:* Amazon and Orinoco basins. *Diet:* Small live fish, beef heart, food fish.

WHITE SPOT: *see* DISEASES OF TROPICAL FISH.

WHITEWORM (*Enchytraeus albidus*): a relative of the common earthworm much used as a food for aquarium fish. Easily cultivated by the home aquarist in commercially prepared compounds or sterilized mixtures of peat, soil, and sand, whiteworms have an exceedingly high fat content and should not exclusively comprise the diet of any tropical fish.

WORM CATARACT: *see* DISEASES OF TROPICAL FISH.

WRASSE: any of numerous, chiefly tropical, often vividly colored marine fishes of the family Labridae, of which such examples as the YELLOWTAIL WRASSE (*Coris gaimardi*) are extremely popular with saltwater aquarists.

X-RAY FISH or **PRISTELLA** (*Pristella riddlei*): One of the most popular freshwater tropicals, this small tetra is peaceable, active, attractive, and makes itself highly visible. The body is silvery and somewhat translucent with yellowish tints, the caudal fin is red and the dorsal and anal fins are marked with black, while the anal fin of the male is further embellished with a white leading edge. *Habitat:* Northeastern South America. *Diet:* Standard aquarium foods, with live foods preferred.

YELLOW-EDGED APHYOSEMION (*Roloffia petersi* or *Aphyosemion petersi*): This peaceful little killifish, one of the plainer of the Aphyosemions, bears faint red dots on an olive-to-brown body. The male, at about 2½ inches, is slightly larger than the female. *Habitat:* Coastal and eastern tropical Africa. *Diet:* Small live foods.

YELLOW-FINNED LAMPEYE (*Aplocheilichthys flavipinnis*): Although its life span is quite short, this diminutive killifish breeds rapidly. Yellow-bodied with a greenish shimmer, the fish has blue-edged yellow dorsal and anal fins. *Habitat:* Nigeria. *Diet:* Small live foods exclusively. NOTE: Best kept in schools and not well-suited to community aquaria.

X-ray Fish

Yellowtail Wrasse

YELLOWHEAD JAWFISH (*Opisthoganthus aurifons*): In nature, this small, blunt-headed marine fish burrows deep into the sea bed, lines the entrance to its tunnel with pebbles to shore it up against cave-ins, and is quite fierce in the defence of its nest. Silver-blue with a yellow-flushed head, it is known for its tendency to "stand" or "dance" on its tail. *Habitat:* Florida Keys, West Indies. *Diet:* Chopped shrimp, frozen brine shrimp. NOTE: Uneaten food should not be allowed to accumulate on the tank bottom.

YELLOW-TAILED AFRICAN CHARACIN (*Alestopetersius caudalus*): Small and silver-gray, the male of the species has lemon-yellow finnage, with a black streak dividing the lobes of the caudal fin. Peaceable with fishes its own size or larger, it should be kept in a covered tank. *Habitat:* Congo River region. *Diet:* Small live foods, with prepared foods taken reluctantly.

YELLOWTAIL WRASSE (*Coris gaimardi*): This hardy, popular marine fish is seen at its best when young, while its body is still a deep red set off by slashlike white markings, outlined in black, on its back.

As the fish matures, the red coloration is superseded by a motley of blues, greens, and yellows. *Habitat:* Tropical Pacific waters. *Diet:* Finely chopped shrimp and the smaller live foods.

YELLOW TANG (1) or **BLUE TANG** (*Acanthrus coeruleus*): a largely herbaceous marine fish that does not thrive well in captivity, it is a vivid sulphur-yellow, spade-shaped, and has a narrow protuberant snout. As the fish matures, its yellow coloration turns deep blue. *Habitat:* Offshore Florida West Indies waters. *Diet:* Dry foods, small live foods, chopped shrimp, algae. (2) *Zebrasoma flavescens*, a vivid yellow Pacific marine fish with a projecting snout. *Habitat:* Hawaii to the East Indies. *Diet:* Varied meaty foods.

YELLOW TETRA (*Hyphessobrycon bifasciatus*): Well-suited to community aquaria, this hardy, easily bred little characin is among the least colorful of the tetras and therefore not very popular with aquarists. Yellow-bodied and somewhat iridescent, it bears two indistinct vertical streaks on the shoulder. *Habitat:* Southern coast of Brazil. *Diet:* Omnivorous; most standard foods taken greedily.

Z

ZANCLIDAE: the taxonomic family comprised of a single species, the MOORISH IDOL (*Zanclus cornutus* or *Z. canescens*).

ZEBRA CICHLID: *see* CONVICT CICHLID.

ZEBRA DANIO or **ZEBRA FISH** (*Brachydanio rerio*): Well-marked, extremely active, and altogether peaceable, this is an enormously popular fish, particularly with beginning aquarists. Silver-gray with well-defined horizontal blue-black stripes, it breeds readily and is easily maintained. *Habitat:* Eastern India. *Diet:* Varied standard aquarium foods.

INDEX OF SCIENTIFIC NAMES

A

Abudefduf:
  caeruleus—blue demoiselle or blue damselfish
  saxtilis—sergeant major

Acanthodoras spinosissimus—spiny catfish or talking catfish

Acanthophthalmus:
  javanicus—Javanese loach
  kuhlii—coolie (or kuhlii) loach
  semicinctus—half-banded loach

Acanthurus:
  coeruleus—yellow tang
  leucosternon—powder-blue surgeon fish
  unicolor—Atlantic yellow tang (see surgeon fish)

Acaronia nassa—big-eyed cichlid

Adioryx diadema—barred squirrelfish (see squirrelfish)

Aequidens:
  curviceps—flag cichlid or Thayer's cichlid
  itanyi—dolphin cichlid
  maroni—keyhole cichlid
  portalegrensis—black acara or port acara
  pulcher—blue acara
  tetramerus—pishuna

Alestes:
  longipinnis—African tetra
  nurse—nurse tetra
  taeniurus—African tetra

Alestopetersius caudalus—yellow-tailed African characin

Amblydoras hancockii—Hancock's amblydoras

Amia calva—bowfin, mudfish, or dogfish

Amphiprion percula or *A. sebae*—clown anemone or anemone fish

Anabas testudineus—climbing perch

Ancistrus lineolatus—bristle-nose

Angelichthys:
  cilaris—blue angelfish
  isabelita—queen angelfish
  townsendi—Townsend angelfish

Anistoremus virginicus—porkfish

Anoptichthys jordani—blind cave characin or blind cave fish

Anostomus anostomus—striped headstander

Antennarius scaber—anglerfish

Apeltes quadracus—stickleback

Aphanius fasciatus—banded minnow

Aphyocharax rubripinnis—bloodfin

Aphyocypris pooni—white cloud mountain minnow

Amphyosemion:
  arnoldi—Arnold's lyretail
  australe—lyretail or lyretailed panchax
  bertholdi—Berthold's killie
  calliurum ahli—Ahl's aphyosemion
  calliurum c.—blue calliurum
  cinnamomeum—cinnamon killie
  coeruleum—blue gularis
  gery—Gery's aphyosemion
  labarrei—Labarre's aphyosemion
  petersi—yellow-edged aphyosemion
  sjoestedti—former scientific name of golden pheasant or golden pheasant gularis (*Roloffia occidentalis*)

Apistogramma:
  agassizai—Agassiz's dwarf cichlid
  ambloplitoides—Peruvian dwarf cichlid
  borelli—umbrella dwarf cichlid
  klausewitzi—Klausewitz' dwarf cichlid
  pertense—Amazon dwarf cichlid
  ramirezi—Ramirez' dwarf cichlid or ram

Aplocheilichthys:
  flavipinnis—yellow-finned lampeye
  katangae—Katanga lampeye
  macrophthalmus—lamp-eye
  myersi—hummingbird fish or Myers' lampeye

Aplocheilus:
  dayi—Ceylon panchax or Day's panchax
  panchax—blue panchax

Apogon maculatus—cardinal fish

Apteronotus albifrons—black ghost

Arnoldichthys spilopterus—Arnold's characin or red-eyed characin

Artemia salina—brine shrimp

Astronotus ocellatus—oscar or marbled cichlid

Axelrodia riesei—ruby tetra

B

Badis:
  badis—badis or dwarf chameleon fish
  badis burmanicus—Burmese badis

Balantiocheilus melanopterus—bala shark

Balistapus undulatus—undulate triggerfish or orange-striped triggerfish

Balistes vetula—queen triggerfish

Balistoides niger—clown triggerfish

Barbodes:
  binotatus—spotted barb
  camptacanthus—African red-finned barb
  everetti—clown barb
  fasciatus—striped barb
  lateristriga—spanner barb or T-barb
  schwanenfeldi—tinfoil barb

Barbus:
  fasciatus—striped barb
  hexazona—six-banded barb

Bathethiops fowleri—African moonfish

Belonesox belizanus—pike top minnow or pike livebearer

Belontia signata—comb-tail paradise fish or comb-tail

Betta:
  brederi—Breder's betta
  splendens—betta or Siamese fighting fish; varietal, split-tailed betta

184

Bodianus:
   pulchellus—hogfish, commonly called scarlet or Cuban hogfish
   rufus—hogfish, commonly called Spanish hogfish

Botia:
   beauforti—Beaufort's loach
   horae—Hora's loach
   hymenophysa—banded loach
   lucas-bahi—barred loach
   macracantha—clown loach or tiger botia

Brachydanio:
   albolineatus—pearl danio
   frankei—leopard danio
   nigrofasciatus—spotted danio
   rerio—zebra danio or zebra fish

Brachygobius:
   aggregatus—Philippine bumblebee
   xanthozona—bumblebeefish

C

Callichthys callichthys—armored catfish

Capoeta:
   arulius—longfin barb
   chola—swamp barb
   oligolepis—checkered barb or checker barb
   semifasciolatus—half-banded barb
   tetrazona—tiger barb or Sumatra barb
   titteya—cherry barb

Carassius auratus—goldfish; varietals, celestial goldfish, comet goldfish, eggfish, fantail goldfish, lionhead goldfish, shubunkin, telescope fantail goldfish, and many others

Centropyge argi—cherubfish

Chaetodon:
   capistratus—four-eyed butterfly fish
   striatus—banded butterfly fish
   trifasciatus—redfin butterfly fish

Chanda lala—glassfish

Channallabes apus—eel catfish

Cheirodon axelrodi—cardinal tetra

Chelmon rostratus—copperband butterfly fish or longnose Australian butterfly

Chilodus punctatus—spotted headstander

Chilomycterus schoepfii—spiny boxfish

Chromis marginatus—blue reef fish

Cichlasoma:
   biocellatum—Jack Dempsey
   erythraeum—red devil
   facetum—chanchito or chanchita
   meeki—fire-mouth or fire-mouth cichlid
   nigrofasciatum—convict cichlid or zebra cichlid
   ostofasciatum—Jack Dempsey

Cirrhitichthys aprinus—spotted hawkfish (see hawkfish)

Cobitis taenia—spotted weatherfish or spined loach

Colisa:
   chunae—honey gourami, honey dwarf gourami, or sunset gourami
   fasciata—giant gourami or striped gourami
   labiosa—thick-lipped gourami
   lalia-dwarf gourami

Colomesus psittacus—South American puffer

Copeina arnoldi—jumping characin, spraying characin, or splash tetra

Coris gaimardi—yellowtail wrasse

Corydoras:
   aeneus—Aeneus catfish or bronze catfish
   agassizai—Agassiz's catfish
   ambiacus—Agassiz's catfish
   cochui—Cochu's catfish
   julii—leopard catfish or leopard corydoras
   microps—wavy catfish
   myersi—Myers' catfish
   undulatus—wavy catfish

Corydorus aeneus—albino corydorus (see albino)

Corynopoma riisei—swordtail characin

Corythoichthys albirostris—pipefish

Crenicara maculata—checkerboard cichlid

Crenicichla:
   geayi—half-banded pike cichlid
   lepidota—pike cichlid

Ctenopoma ansorgei—ornate ctenopoma

Ctenops vittatus—croaking gourami

Cynolebias nigripinnis—black-finned pearl fish or dwarf Argentine pearlfish

Cynopoecilus ladigesi—Ladies' gaucho

Cyprinus carpio—carp

D

Danio malabaricus—giant danio

Dascyllus melanurus—black-tailed dascyllus or black-tailed humbug

Dantnioides quadrifasciatus—four-barred tiger fish

Dermgenys pusillus—half-beak

Diodon hystrix—porcupine fish

Dormitator maculatus—sleeper goby or spotted sleeper

Dytiscus marginalis—great diving beetle

E

Elassoma everngladei—pygmy sunfish

Enchytraeus buchholtzi—grindal worm

Enneacanthus gloriosus—diamond sunfish

Epalzeorhynchus kallopterus—flying fox

Epinephelus adscensionis—rock hind

Epeplatys:
   annulatus—clown killie
   chaperi—fire-mouth panchax or redjaw killie
   dageti monroviae—Arnold's killie

Equetus:
  acuminatus—chubbyu or high hat
  lanceolatus—ribbon fish or jacknife fish

Esomus danrica or *E. danricus*—flying barb

Etroplus maculatus—orange chromide or
  orange cichlid

G

Gambusia afinis a. or *Gambusia afinis
holbooki*—mosquito fish

Gammarus pulex—freshwater shrimp

Gasterosteus aculeatus—stickleback

Geophagus jurupari—demon fish, jurupari, or
  eartheater

Gephyrocharax caucanus—arrowhead tetra

Ginglymostoma cirratum—nurse shark

Glaridichthys falcatus—mosquito fish

Gobiosoma oceanops—neon goby

Gobius sadanundio—knight goby

Gramma loretto—royal gramma

Gymnocorymbus ternetzi and *G. thayeri*
  —black tetra

Gymnothorax nigromarginatus—black-edge
  moray (see moray)

Gymnotus carapo—banded knife fish or
  sarapo

Gyrinocheilus aymonieri—chinese algae-
  eater

H

Halichores bivittatus—Slippery Dick

Haplochromis multicolor—Egyptian mouthbreeder (or mouthbrooder)

Helostoma rudolfi—kissing gourami

Hemichromis bimaculatus—jewel cichlid or
  red cichlid

Hemigrammus:
  erythrozonus or *gracilis*—glowlight tetra
  hyanuary—January tetra
  nanus—silver-tip tetra
  ocellifer—head-and-tail-light
  pulcher—garnet tetra

Hemiodus semitaeniatus—half-lined hemiodus

Hericthys cyanoguttatus—Rio Grande perch
  or Texas cichlid

Heterandria formosa—mosquito fish

Hippasteria spinosa—starfish

Hippocampus zosterae—pygmy sea horse or
  dwarf sea horse

Histrio histrio—sargassum fish

Holocanthus:
  ciliaris—queen angel fish
  tricolor—rock beauty

Hoplosternum littorale—cascudo or hoplo

Hyphessobrycon:
  bifasciatus—yellow tetra
  callistus callistus—callistus tetra or serpa
   tetra
  innesi—neon tetra
  peruvianus—loreto tetra
  pulchripinnis—lemon tetra
  rosaceus—rosy tetra or black flag
  rubrostigma—bleeding heart tetra or tetra
   perez
  scholzei—black-lined tetra
  serpae—tetra serpae

Hypoplectrus unicolor—butter hamlet

Hypostomus plecostomus—sucker catfish

J

Jordanella floridae—American flagfish

Julidochromis ornatus—julie

K

Kryptopterus bicirrhis—glass catfish

L

Labeo bicolor—red-tailed shark

Lactinius oceanops—neon goby

Ladigesia roloffi—jellybean tetra

Lamprologus leleupi—lemon cichlid

Laubuca:
  dadiburjori—dadio
  laubuca—Indian hatchetfish

Lebistes reticulatus—guppy; varietals, golden
  double sword guppy, green lace guppy,
  scarf-tail guppy, veiltail guppy, and many
  others

Lepidarchus adonis—Adonis

Lepomis gibbosus—sunfish or pumpkinseed

Leporinus:
  agassizi—half-striped leporinus
  arcus—lipstick leporinus
  fasciatus—banded leporinus
  maculatus—spotted leporinus
  striatus—striped leporinus

Lima scabra—flame scallop (see scallop)

Lima:
  nigrofasciata—humpback limia or hunchback limia
  vittata—banded limia

Loricaria parva—whiptail(ed) catfish or whiptail loricaria

M

Macropodus:
  cupanus dayi—Day's paradise fish
  opercularis—paradise fish

Malapterurus electricus—electric catfish

Mastacembelus armatus and *M. maculatus*
  —spiny eel

Melanotaenia:
  macculochi—dwarf Australian rainbow fish
  nigrans—Australian rainbowfish
Micralestes interruptus—Congo tetra or featherfail tetra
Micropanchax macrophthalmus—lamp-eye
Microspathodon chrysyrus—jewel fish
Mimagoniates:
  barberi—Barber's tetra
  inequalis—croaking tetra
Misgurnus anguillicaudatus—Japanese weatherfish
Moekhausia pittieri—diamond tetra
Mogurnda mogurnda—purple-striped gudgeon
Mollienesia:
  latipinna—sailfin molly
  sphenops—sphenops or molly
Monocirrhus polyacanthus—leaf fish
Monodactylus argenteus—Malayan angel, fingerfish, or mono
Morulius chrysophekadion—black shark

N

Nannacara anomala—golden-eyed dwarf cichlid
Nannaethiops tritaeniatus and *N. unitaeniatus*—African tetra
Nannobrycon espei—barred pencilfish
Nannochromis dimidiatus—dimidiatus
Nannostomus:
  anomalus—anomalous pencilfish
  aripirangensis—aripiranga pencilfish
  espei—barred pencilfish
Nematobrycon:
  amphiloxus—rainbow tetra
  palmeri—emperor tetra
Neolebias:
  ansorgei—Ansorge's neolebias
  landgrafi—blue-banded neolebias
Neomacheilus fasciatus—barred loach
Nomeus gronovii—man-of-war fish
Nothobranchius melanospilus—beira nothobranch

O

Opisthoganthus aurifons—yellowhead jaw fish
Oryzias:
  javanicus—Java killie or Javanese rich fish
  latipes—medaka or rice fish
Osphronemus goramy—gourami
Osteochilus hasselti—hard-lipped barb
Osteoglossum:
  bicirrhosum—arowana
  ferreirai—black arowana
Otocinclus arnoldi—Arnold's sucker catfish

Oxyeleotris marmoratus—marbled goby
Oxymonacanthus
  longirostris—orange-spotted filefish or longnosed filefish

P

Panchax chaperi—fire-mouth panchax or red-jaw killie
Pantadon buchholzi—butterfly fish
Paracirrhites forsteri—freckled hawkfish (see hawkfish)
Parauchenoglanis macrostoma—African spotted catfish
Pedalibrycon felipponei—Uruguay characin
Periophthalmus:
  barbarus—mudskipper
  papilio—butterfly mudskipper
Petrotilapia tridentiger—blue petrotilapia
Phallichthys amates—merry widow
Phenacogrammus interruptus—Congo tetra or featherfail tetra
Phoxinus phoxinus—minnow and numrous killifish species
Phractura ansorgei—African whiptailed catfish
Planorbis corneus—red ramshorn
Plantax:
  orbicularis or *pinnatus*—batfish
  pinnatus—orange-ringed batfish or long-finned batfish
Plecostomus bolivianus—Bolivian sucker catfish
Poecilia:
  latipinna—sailfin molly
  mexicana—sphenops or molly
  vittata—banded limia
Poecilobrycon espei—barred pencilfish
Polyacanthus dayi—Day's paradise fish
Polycentropis abbreviata—African leaf fish
Pomacanthus:
  arcuatus—black angelfish or gray angelfish
  imperator—emperor angelfish
  maculosus—half-moon angelfish
  paru—French angelfish
  semicirculatus—Pacific blue angelfish (see blue angelfish)
  semicirculatus—koran or koran angelfish
Pomacentrus leucostictus—beau gregory
Prionobrama filigera—translucent bloodfin or glass bloodfin
Pristella riddlei—x-ray fish or pristella
Pterois volitans—lionfish, turkeyfish, or cobra fish
Pterolebias peruensis—Peruvian longfin
Pterophyllum altum, P. eimekei, or *P. scalare*—angelfish, varietal, veil angelfish (*P. scalare*)

Puntius:
    conchonius—rosy barb
    filamentosus—black-spot barb
    saschi—golden barb
    ticto—two-spot barb or tic-tac-toe barb
    wohlerti—sickle barb

Pygocentrus calmoni—dusky piranha

Pygoplites diacanthus—regal angelfish

Pyrrhulina:
    filamentosa—jumping characin, spraying characin, or splash tetra
    vittata—banded pyrrhulina

Q

Quintana atrizon—black-barred livebearer

R

Rasbora:
    einthoveni—brilliant rasbora or Einthoven's rasbora
    heteromorpha—harlequin fish
    maculata—spotted rasbora or pygmy rasbora
    trilineata—scissortail rasbora
    urophthalma—exclamation-point rasbora or ocellated dwarf rasbora
    vaterifloris—Ceylonese fire barb

Rivulus:
    cylindraceus—Cuban rivulus
    harti—Hart's rivulus
    urophthalmus—golden rivulus (see Hart's rivulus)

Roloffia:
    occidentalis—golden pheasant or golden pheasant gularis
    petersi—yellow-edged aphyosemion

S

Scatophagus argus—spotted scat

Selene vomer—lookdown

Serrasalmus nattereri—Natterer's piranha or red-bellied piranha

Serrasalmus rhombeus—white piranha or spotted piranha

Sorubim lima—shovel-nose catfish

Sphaerichthys osphromenoides—chocolate gourami

Steatocranus casuarius—lionhead cichlid

Stenopus hispidus—banded coral shrimp

Sternarchus albifrons—black ghost

Symphysodon:
    aequifasciata a.—green discus
    discus—red discus or pompadou

Syngnathus pulchellus—African freshwater pipefish (see pipefish)

Synodontis:
    angelicus—polka dot African catfish
    davidi—David's upside-down catfish
    nigriventris—upside-down catfish

T

Tanichthys albonubes—white cloud minnow

Teleogramma brichardi—Brichard's African dwarf cichlid

Telmatherina ladigesi—Celebes sailfin or Celebes rainbow fish

Tetraodon:
    cutcutia—common pufferfish or Maylayan puffer
    miurus—Congo puffer

Therapon jarbua—jarbua or target fish

Tilapia:
    mossambica—Mozambique cichlid or Mozambique tilapia
    sparrmani—peacock cichlid

Toxotes jaculator—archer fish

Trichogaster:
    leeri—pearl gourami, mosaic gourami, or leeri
    pectoralis—snakeskin gourami
    trichopterus—blue gourami
    trichopterus—three-spot gourami

Trichopsis vittatus—croaking gourami

Triportheus elongatus—elongated hatchetfish

X

Xenocara dolichoptera—bushy-mouthed catfish

Xiphophorus:
    helleri—swordtail, sword, or helleri; varietals: green swordtail, Simpson swordtail or Simpson hi-fin sword
    Maculatus—platy or moonfish; varietals: golden wagtail, wagtail platy (aquarium bred)
    montezumae—Mexican swordtail
    variatus—variegated platy

Z

Zanclus canescens or *Z. cornutus*—Moorish idol

Zebrasoma:
    flavescens—yellow tang
    veliferum—sailfiin tang

BIBLIOGRAPHY

H.R. Axelrod and W.E. Burgess. *Saltwater Aquarium Fish*. T.F.H. Publications, 1973.

H.R. Axelrod and W. Vorderwinkler. *Encyclopedia of Tropical Fishes*. T.F.H. Publications, 1969.

Axelrod, Vorderwinkler, et al. *Exotic Tropical Fishes*. T.F.H. Publications, 1962.

C.M. Breder, Jr. *Field Book of Marine Fishes of the Atlantic Coast*. G.P. Putnam's Sons, 1948.

C.W. Coates. *Tropical Fish as Pets*. Liveright, 1950.

A. Cooper. *Fishes of the World*. Grosset & Dunlap, 1971.

G. Cust and P. Bird. *Tropical Freshwater Aquaria*. Grosset & Dunlap, 1971.

H. Frey. *Illustrated Dictionary of Tropical Fishes*. T.F.H. Publications, 1961.

G.F. Hervey and J. Hems. *Freshwater Tropical Aquarium Fishes*. Spring Books, 1965.

W.T. Innes. *Exotic Aquarium Fishes*. Metaframe/Dutton, 1966.

A. Nieuwenhuizen. *Tropical Aquarium Fish: Their Habits and Breeding Behavior*. Van Nostrand, 1964.

R.P.L. Straughan. *The Salt Water Aquarium in the Home*. A.S. Barnes, 1972.

F. Yasuda, Y. Hiyama, et al. *Pacific Marine Fishes*. T.F.H. Publications, 1972.

The Complete Aquarist's Guide to Freshwater Tropical Fishes. Golden Press, 1970.

PHOTO CREDITS: *J. Crook* p. 65. *Free-lance Photographers Guild, Inc.* p. 136–137. *National Audubon Society* p. 79 (t.) John H. Gerard; p. 80 (t.) John H. Gerard; p. 80 (bot.) Berty Barford. *Photo Researchers, Inc.* p. 81 Tom Mc Hugh; p. 135 Russ Kinne; p. 159 Russ Kinne.